Cemeteries of Caroline County Virginia

VOLUME 1
PUBLIC CEMETERIES

Compiled by
Herbert Ridgeway Collins

HERITAGE BOOKS
2009

HERITAGE BOOKS

AN IMPRINT OF HERITAGE BOOKS, INC.

Books, CDs, and more—Worldwide

For our listing of thousands of titles see our website
at
www.HeritageBooks.com

Published 2009 by
HERITAGE BOOKS, INC.
Publishing Division
100 Railroad Ave. #104
Westminster, Maryland 21157

Other books by the author:

Caroline County, Virginia Bureau of Vital Statistics: Death Records, 1853-1896

Caroline County, Virginia Death Records (1919-1994) from
The Caroline Progress, *a Weekly Newspaper Published in Bowling Green, Virginia*

Cemeteries of Caroline County, Virginia, Volumes 1–3: Public Cemeteries

Cover photograph: St. Peter's Episcopal Church, Port Royal, Virginia. Built in 1835, this is the oldest Episcopal church in continuous use in Caroline County.

International Standard Book Numbers
Paperbound: 978-1-58549-362-3
Clothbound: 978-0-7884-8215-1

TABLE OF CONTENTS

LIST OF ILLUSTRATIONS

INTRODUCTION

This volume consists of information that was primarily gathered from cemeteries in Caroline County, Virginia which were visited by the compiler in the early 1960's. There has been no attempt made to bring it up to date, since the period from the 1960's to the present has little genealogical meaning. After the material was originally copied, graves have been moved, some from other church or private cemeteries to new locations. In 1994, the compiler revisited Lakewood Cemetery, Shiloh Methodist Church, Salem Baptist Church, Bethel Baptist Church, Bethel Methodist Church, Bethany Baptist Church, Carmel Baptist Church, Concord Baptist Church, and Mount Hermon Baptist Church, and made adjustments accordingly.

In some cases, graves were only marked with temporary metal markers used by funeral directors at the time of interment. Some of these were faded so they were illegible. In cases where a husband and wife shared a stone, and one was alive at the time of the original survey in the 1960's, a date of death will be missing here. In most cases, the inscriptions were copied in the order they appear in the cemetery. Because of the presentation format in this publication, some inscriptions cannot be given exactly as they are found.

When the Government established Greenlawn Cemetery, it used small bronze plates to mark all the graves which did not have existing stones when they were moved from other locations. Small bronze markers were placed at each grave, but since many were not anchored, they have shifted from lawn mowing. Others have been broken, and some were removed entirely when permanent stone monuments were added.

The oldest inscriptions are found in Greenlawn Cemetery. These are graves moved by the government in 1940-1941 from private cemeteries at homesites rather than church cemeteries in that area. The earliest of these dates from 1760 on the Buckner property. Since they now rest in a public cemetery, they are included in this work.

The Presbyterians began worship in Caroline County as early as the 1740's, first at old Needwood Tavern and later at a site nearby. Today there is an active congregation at Milford, where they have occupied two different buildings since 1909. There is no known burying ground for that congregation. The places of burial at most of the original colonial parish churches in the County were destroyed years ago and what tombstones which once existed have been carried away. There is record of a grave of Lady Buckner who was buried under the steps of Old Mount Church, but when that church was converted to Rappahannock Academy in the 19th Century, some of the students vandalized the grave. It is unfortunate that information on burials at these ancient churches has been lost to history. I hope we look more kindly toward the present and deal with history in a more positive and constructive way.

There was a church cemetery in back of the Bowling Green Baptist Church, North Main Street, which included a childs grave and some five or six adult graves—some of which were members of Josh Williams' family. It is unfortunate that these graves have been destroyed and the stones recently moved from the site.

In closing, a few acknowledgements are in order. First and foremost, Wesley E. Pippenger of Arlington, an authority on this subject, having himself having had published four volumes covering tombstone inscriptions in Alexandria, as well as other notable publications. His expertise and encouragement has been invaluable. Most of all, I am indebted to him for having formatted and typed this manuscript.

Others who have assisted include Mr. and Mrs. Lloyd Covington of "Ruther Glen," who provided information concerning the history of St. Paul's Methodist Church, and Miss Mary Elizabeth Pitts of Sparta, who not only inspired me as teacher and librarian when I attended high school in Caroline County but who provided insight on the site of Old Salem Baptist Church. Also, I am indebted to Elizabeth J. Furr, Kathryn Davis Burchell and William L. Gravatt, Jr. for their assistance in compiling the section of this work concerning undertakers in Caroline.

As in every study, it is impossible to include all the interesting facets. In this case, it is regrettable that the artwork of the stones and epitaphs cannot be included, for these make touring old cemeteries so special.

Herbert Ridgeway Collins
"Green Falls"
Caroline County
1994

UNDERTAKERS OF CAROLINE COUNTY

During the 19th Century, most funerals were conducted from the home of the deceased or from their church. Embalming was not done beyond packing the deceased in ice or liberally using arsenic which could delay the burial a day or two to allow relatives and loved ones to assemble. Graves were dug by a local grave digger, and coffins were made by someone local. My great-great grandfather, James F. Campbell, made many coffins during his lifetime. When someone died in the community, he took a long stick to the residence to measure the corpse. He made the coffins of 12-inch wide boards, and covered then with paint that was made by burning thick poplar bark and mixing the ashes with sweet milk. He then lined the coffins with cheesecloth purchased from the local store. By the late 19th Century, various country stores began handling coffins as well as groceries and other goods. Some individuals would not buy groceries from these stores because they sold coffins.

Edmund Pendleton died in Richmond, Virginia on October 23, 1803. The funeral arrangements were made by a Richmond undertaker. A service was held there where the crowd followed a horse-drawn hearse to the northern outskirts of town, after which mourners returned while the hearse traveled some 40 miles to Pendleton's home "Edmundsbury," in Caroline County for the interment in the cemetery behind the house. With advent of the railroad in the mid-19th Century, bodies could be transported by rail as could coffins from the undertakers in the surrounding metropolitan areas. In many instances in the rural areas, even up into the 20th Century, a mule and a wagon transported the remains from the home to the burial site. Such was the case as late as 1925 when Eugene B. Jeter was buried at Emmaus Christian Church.

Funeral homes in nearby Ashland, Richmond and Fredericksburg have also served the County since the end of the 19th Century. In many instances the case and box was purchased from a funeral home outside the area and transported by a horse-drawn vehicle and later by train to the home of the deceased. In these cases the funeral home had nothing more to do with the funeral. Such was the circumstance for Mary Dorothea Buckner Wright who died January 16, 1889. The next day, her nephew purchased for $25 a case and box from L.T. Christian Funeral Home at 1215 E. Broad Street, Richmond, and transported it to the residence. In 1932, Elkins Funeral Home in Fredericksburg provided a casket and hearse service for the same family at a cost of $90 for the complete package.

There is no record of an undertaker in Caroline County before the 20th Century. The first one for which there is a record was operated by Hugh M. Pegg, who first operated a carriage and wagon maker's business and later operated as an undertaker at the site on Chase Street across from the present day Masonic lodge building in Bowling Green. The site is now part of a county parking lot. Pegg was operating on this site on January 19, 1907, when he had the distinction of removing the remains of Edmund Pendleton and his two wives and infant son from the home at "Edmundsbury," near File, Caroline County, to the aisle of Bruton Parish Church in Williamsburg.

The second funeral home was located at the corner of Chase and Main streets in Bowling Green, on the site earlier occupied by William Wright's carriage and wagon factory. Today, a Texaco service station occupies the site. This funeral home was operated by John Gill sometime prior to December 27, 1924, when he handled the funeral of John Lawrence Jordan who was buried in Lakewood Cemetery. His advertisement first appears in The Caroline Progress newspaper on March 13, 1925, as *John W. Gill - Bowling Green - Funeral Director - Dealer in General Merchandise, Hardware, Sherman-Williams and Wilson Heaters*. His wife, Cora Covington Gill ran a hat shop in Bowling Green. Mr. Gill continued in the funeral business with advertisements in the county newspaper on a regular basis in the 1920's and early 1930's. He died in 1936, and was buried in Lakewood Cemetery at Bowling Green.

Mr. Pegg continued in the funeral business during most of the first half of the 20th Century, and was joined by L.R. "Jack" Davis who had been operating a mercantile business on Main Street in Bowling Green from which he also sold coffins. Mr. Davis bought into the business in the 1930's. The firm was then known as Davis-Pegg Funeral Home, and operations moved to a new brick building erected by Jack Davis in 1941. The building, located next to the Bowling Green Baptist Church, was occupied as the home of Jack Davis who used the parlor of the house for his funeral business. The building is across the street from the home of Mr. and Mrs. Pegg. After it ceased to be used for a funeral home it was sold to Frank Beazley who lived the last years of his life there. It is now the office of the Allstate Insurance Company. Mr. Pegg died on May 10, 1940. His wife Sally Ann continued to live in the home until her death at age 89 years on February 27, 1975. Both are buried in unmarked graves adjacent to those of his mother and his brother Wallace Pegg, in graves 5, 6, 7, and 8 in Lot 12, Section E of Lakewood Cemetery, Bowling Green.

In March 1928, both John W. Gill, funeral director, and the firm known as "Davis and Pegg, Undertakers" had their advertisements in the county newspaper. Later, Pegg's association with Davis ceased and the name Davis Funeral Home was used until 1947 when the business was sold to Paul W. Manns. Davis Funeral Home had charge of moving the graves from private family burying grounds and church cemeteries in the area encompassed by Camp A.P. Hill (later changed to Fort A.P. Hill) to the newly-formed Greenlawn Cemetery. Only eight graves were moved to other cemeteries: four to Salem Baptist Church, and four to Lakewood Cemetery. Joe Ayers supervised the moving for Jack Davis. "Red" Ayers helped in transporting remains to the new location, and John Crowell assisted in the removal. The remains were all placed in grey-painted wood boxes. The records of this procedure, complete with drawings, are preserved. The originals of these are with the Caroline Historical Society. Jack Davis sold the funeral business shortly after the war but continued to live in the county until his death on August 21, 1971, at the age of 65 years. He is buried in Greenlawn Cemetery.

Paul W. Manns, who purchased the Davis funeral business, also owned and purchased the local newspaper which had previously been operated by Davis. Manns served as a state senator and as editor of the newspaper while also being an undertaker. He ran the funeral home out of the house known as the old Wright home, which had been the residence of William Wright, who operated a wagon and carriage factory on the site next door, and where John Gill had his funeral business. The Wright home served as the funeral home for years, and Paul W. Manns and his family lived in the upstairs of the house.

In the 1950's, Mr. Hoy joined Manns as partner, again causing a change in the firm's name, this time to Manns-Hoy Funeral Home. Hoy severed partnership with Senator Manns and purchased the Athol Collins property across the street, between the Episcopal and Methodist churches. He moved the Collins house to the side street, converted it into apartments, and made plans to build a funeral home on its former site. These plans never materialized, and Mr. Hoy moved from Caroline.

In 1968, Mr. Manns renovated the old Safeway store adjacent to the Wright home where he was operating and then moved into the new accommodations. This building offered air conditioning, with a spacious chapel and family room. In 1979, the business was sold by Mr. Manns to Dr. W. Allen Powell, and the name was changed to Manns-Powell, subsequently Powell Funeral Home. Eight years later, David W. Storke became funeral director there and purchased the business on May 30, 1991. The business has been known as Storke Funeral Home since 1993. Mr. Manns continued to live in Caroline County where he died on March 16, 1978, aged 68, and was buried in Lakewood Cemetery.

John Broaddus Gravatt, son of William Broaddus and Mary Jane Chapman Gravatt, ran a grist mill and farm in King William County. He also had a blacksmith and carpenter's shop next to "Bleak Hill." He started making coffins in his shop and later expanded into the funeral business. In 1935, he relocated to Caroline County and built the Gravatt Funeral Home next door to the old Dawn post office on Route 30, across from the old Dawn school. Mr. Gravatt and his son William L. "Willie" Gravatt operated the business together until it closed around 1952. John Broaddus Gravatt died January 15, 1958, and his son Willie died on December 31, 1967. Both are buried in Forest Lawn Cemetery in Richmond. William L. "Billy" Gravatt, Jr., who lives in Richmond, now possesses the records of the funeral home.

Antioch Christian Church

Antioch Christian Church

Antioch Christian Church, located on Main Street in Bowling Green, Virginia, across the street from St. Asaph's Episcopal Church, has occupied six different buildings. The first building, was of frame construction and was destroyed by fire. The second building, located on the same site at Antioch Fork where the Milford Road (now Antioch Road) intersects with U.S. Route 2, was built of brick. The congregation sold that building and it was later crafted into a residence, the windows being partially bricked to make them shorter. This is now the residence of Mr. and Mrs. Lewis Gravatt.

The third church building, which was located on the site of the present building, was of frame construction and was erected about 1847. It burned on February 21, 1986. The fourth church building, constructed with a slate roof, contained the Dickinson Memorial window which was dedicated on December 4, 1887. The building burned in Spring 1892, destroying the memorial window. The fifth building which was erected that year was struck by lightening and burned on July 9, 1917. The present structure was built on the original site in Bowling Green in 1920. There is a memorial window in the present building which commemorates Algernon B. Chandler, an early pillar of the church.

In a copy of A Memorial Sermon of Festus and Elizabeth B. Dickinson, printed by the Free Lance newspaper of Fredericksburg, for the dedication of the memorial window, we find two other graves cited which are now in the field in back of the Raines' house next door.

A beautiful shaft of parian marble, enclosed by marble posts and galvanized iron railings, erected by Col. A.G. Dickinson, their son, in recent years, marks the spot in the rear of Antioch Church, Bowling Green, where the remains of Mr. Festus Dickinson and his wife are interred.

Mr. Dickinson was born in the year 1795, and his wife in 1804. They were united in marriage in 1820; the groom was twenty-five years of age, the bride sixteen years old. In 1843, Mrs. Dickinson died and her husband survived her about a year.

In back of the present church building and to the right is a single stone surrounded by an iron fence. The stone contains the following inscription:

Rev. John G. Parrish
July 30, 1871, in his 54th year

Nannie Jackson
daughter of Rev. John G. & Betty Bunbury Parrish
Died December 24, 1869, in the 8th year of her age

Betty Bunbury, wife of John G. Parrish
May 28, 1855, in her 41st year of age

This site was visited in 1963.

Bethany Baptist Church

Located off U.S. Route 1 at Nancy Wright's Corner, and west 1 mile on Marye Road. This church is located on a site which is partially in Caroline County and partially in Spotsylvania County, and has boundary markers to this effect in the cemetery. The congregation was first organized in 1770. It was initially known as Guinea's Bridge and was near the village of Guinea. The first meeting house was of frame construction, as was the second and more modest building which was destroyed by fire in 1842. The next year, the church was rebuilt of brick, and it is that structure which stands today. The building was remodeled in 1913, enlarged in 1926, and an educational facility was added in 1968. There are several deeds to the property: 2 acres were acquired on June 4, 1837, 3 acres were added on February 1, 1866, and another addition was made in 1919. The present building is about 100 yards from the original site of Guinea's Bridge. This site was visited in 1962.

CARTER
C. Thelma
Sept. 8, 1930 - Mar. 27, 1961

GATEWOOD
Clifton L.
Nov. 11, 1908 - Apr. 29, 1962

Michael Lewis Durrett
March 4, 1960
March 27, 1960

MARSHALL
R. Mason
Jan. 23, 1934 - Oct. 28, 1958

MARSHALL
Walter Wellington
July 10, 1896 - Nov. 9, 1956
Gracie Clark
July 17, 1897 -

SCOTT
Evangeline A.
July 10, 1895 - July 5, 1953
Lloyd E.
May 20, 1885 - Dec. 19, 1950

Joseph C. Prince
Sept. 18, 1887
June 11, 1941

HOCKADAY
Father
Robert L.
Feb. 18, 1870 - Oct. 5, 1946
Mother
Dora V.
July 22, 1882 - Mar. 28, 1956

HARGRAVE
Charlie M.
July 29, 1876 - Jan. 25, 1948
Annie L.
Oct. 9, 1878 -

CLARK
Joseph A.
Nov. 4, 1896 - Nov. 8, 1956

Glouris W. Stanley
Aug. 22, 1913
Sept. 17, 1957

MARSHALL
Robert A.
June 6, 1883 -
Ila May
May 2, 1886 - Nov. 7, 1948

PFC Willie E. Coleman
Nov. 3, 1924
Aug. 29, 1945

2

GATEWOOD
Clarence H.
1893-
Estelle L.
1900-1958

John Maxwell "Max" Henshaw
May 2, 1943
February 25, 1958

CLARK
Archie S.
1894-1942
Sallie V.
1899-

R. Alfred Blanton
May 26, 1882 - Feb. 24, 1915
Kate D. Blanton
Oct. 16, 1856 - June 17, 1940

RICHESON
W. Henry
Dec. 7, 1866 - Jan. 6, 1946
Judith T.
May 13, 1870 - Jan. 3, 1960

Alice Lee Waller
Born Sept. 1855, Suffolk Co., England
Died March 3, 1936

WALLER
Dabney J.
1879-1959
Minnie L.
1865-1942

HOUCK
William A.
1886-1957
Lila J.
1895-1962
In Memory of our son,
Lt. John Paul Houck,
Pilot, killed in Action
and buried in Hawaii

Bobby H., son of W.A. & L.J. Houck
June 25, 1934 - July 29, 1937

Lynn Mercer Hockaday
Feb. 20, 1909
Sept. 10, 1961

Mother
Elanor Waller Hart
Born June 15, 1911
Died June 15, 1938

I.E.S.

Son James H. Stanley
Mar. 31, 1921
Aug. 28, 1937

William W. Stanley
Sept. 1, 1898
Sept. 28, 1944

Stanley Infants
Angela
1962
Donald
1947

ACORS
Willie L.
Oct. 19, 1889 - July 13, 1958
Mattie
Mar. 5, 1871 - Oct. 22, 1936

Mother
Clara V. Carter
Born June 12, 1893
Died July 6, 1936

Son
Roderick E. Carter
Born Nov. 2, 1917
Died July 12, 1936

Virginia Mae, daughter of
C.A. & Julia McAllister
Jan. 22, 1945 - Apr. 13, 1945

Hugh Mercer Hockaday
Mar. 12, 1876
Oct. 22, 1954

3

Bethany Baptist Church

Lawrence Blanton Durrett
Mar. 25, 1880
Sept. 28, 1958

DURRETT
Robert H.
Mar. 17, 1874 - Jan. 19, 1951
Ashley H.
Feb. 28, 1889 -

CARTER
Richard B.
1858-1923
Mable F.
1884-1961

Infant son of
Aubrey & Patty Young
Dec. 3, 1941

YOUNG
M. Lafayette
Apr. 28, 1877 - Nov. 3, 1939
Cora Mills
Feb. 12, 1881 -

Mother
Mary Elizabeth Acors
Sept. 25, 1868
April 10, 1947

GENTZ
August
1879-1948
Anna
1872-1926
Lewis
1875-1955

Henry L. McAllister
Harts Co.
S.C. Vols.
C.S.A.

Lucy Corr
1870-1939
John Corr
1860-1930
[same info. on headstone and footstone]

BLACKLEY
Walter T.
Aug. 22, 1867 - Mar. 18, 1934
Mary V.
Nov. 10, 1875 -

Virginia B. Usher
daughter of
Mr. & Mrs. R.N. Usher
Aug. 3, 1917 - July 28, 1935

USHER
Robert N.
June 26, 1880 - Mar. 30, 1942
Norma A.
May 16, 1875 - Sept. 20, 1948

James T. Hairfield
Aug. 7, 1879
Nov. 28, 1922

HAIRFIELD
Laura O.
Jan. 20, 1872 - June 29, 1951
James W.
Nov. 17, 1862 - Oct. 18, 1940

Brother
Elwood S. Hairfield
Dec. 16, 1894
Jan. 19, 1958

Willie A. Young
Aug. 13, 1867 - June 18, 1929
Virginia Mills Young
May 16, 1876 - Sept. 6, 1956
Ethel Young Hill
Aug. 23, 1904 - Oct. 18, 1929

A.L.S.

[Handmade stone]
Sadie [Koilliey?]

Catherine M. Hart
wife of William T. Hart
Aug. 8, 1875 - Aug. 8, 1926

4

Bethany Baptist Church

William T. Hart
Co. H, 47 Va. Inf.
C.S.A.

Bettie T. Hart
wife of R.C. Hart
Born Jan. 27, 1844
Died July 12, 1928

Robert C. Hart
Born Aug. 29, 1843
Died Sept. 17, 1934
Co. F, 24 Va. Cav.

Woodrow W. Morris
Dec. 21, 1915
Jan. 13, 1953

Lucy C. Morris
June 4, 1883
Oct. 6, 1951

Mary E. Morris
Aug. 8, 1848
Jan. 11, 1936

Esther E. Morris
Aug. 3, 1908
Jan. 7, 1951

STANLEY
A. Lewis Stanley
Oct. 1, 1864
Apr. 12, 1928

STANLEY
Mary Alice Stanley
Aug. 25, 1868
Oct. 26, 1952

J. Samuel Black
Sept. 13, 1876
May 3, 1946

Joseph A. Black
June 27, 1849
Apr. 27, 1930
Ann C. Black
Oct. 22, 1854
July 5, 1928

Harvey A. Black
Aug. 30, 1883
Oct. 11, 1941

Ruby Mae Morris
Jan. 23, 1917
Dec. 30, 1923

Edward Walter, Jr.
son of E.W. and Cora Morris Attenburg
April 10, 1921
April 21, 1924
Budded on Earth to Bloom in Heaven.

CORR
Charles Lewis Corr
Oct. 25, 1854 - Oct. 3, 1927
His wife
Annie Lively Corr
Dec. 19, 1856 - Oct. 18, 1934

Jack M. Newton
Mar. 31, 1887
Nov. 27, 1961

Maggie L. Newton
wife of R.L. Newton
Oct. 17, 1886
May 16, 1955

BAKER
Cliveus A.
1856-1923
Maria L.
1856-1923

Mother
Rosa Hart Thomas
Aug. 8, 1877 - Nov. 25, 1956

Ruth E., daughter of
B.M. & E.M. Holloway
Oct. 20, 1943 - Oct. 22, 1943

Fannie B. Newton
Mar. 9, 1890
June 10, 1957

Lewis A. Newton
Sept. 2, 1879
Aug. 7, 1947

Ida G. Newton, wife of
J.Z. Newton
Nov. 26, 1851 - Jan. 14, 1929

John Z. Newton
July 26, 1840
Mar. 23, 1893

Thomas H. Newton
Nov. 26, 1875
Dec. 19, 1905

Robert L. Flippo
Jan. 30, 1870
May 10, 1946

Mary L. Flippo
Aug. 1, 1870
Feb. 19, 1936

CORR
Herbert H.
Oct. 2, 1891 - Feb. 2, 1936
Annie R.
Feb. 24, 1890 -

JOHNSON
George B.
Nov. 9, 1881 - Feb. 17, 1941
Julia I.
Oct. 11, 1889 -

WINKLER
Frederick B.
June 5, 1875 - Jan. 4, 1957
Mary E.
Oct. 7, 1879 - Dec. 15, 1958

FLIPPO
Daughter
Minnie
1905-1987
Mother
Kate
1875-1943

Annie R. Faulkner
Mar. 24, 1871
Mar. 26, 1943

[following 6 graves in iron fence with sun
dial in the corner]

Frederick W. Coleman
April 24, 1878 - Feb. 17, 1941
Judge 15th Judicial Circuit, 1925-1941

Edna F. Coleman
Born Feb. 15, 1855
Died April 30, 1920

Robin S. Coleman
June 22, 1882
Sept. 7, 1925

Solon T. Coleman
Feby. 15, 1880
April 1, 1936

Hugh Koren Coleman
July 28, 1876
April 25, 1948

Frederick W. Coleman
Nov. 26, 1915
Sept. 30, 1962

McKENNEY
Louis B.
July 6, 1866 - Feb. 14, 1959
Eva Morris
July 15, 1872 - Nov. 2, 1947

Lester Conway McKenney
Sept. 26, 1914
Apr. 8, 1939

COLEMAN
H.F. Coleman
Apr. 7, 1843 - January 13, 1919
Jennie M. Coleman
June 18, 1845 - October 23, 1931
Emmett M. Coleman
September 7, 1869 - January 9, 1936

6

Bethany Baptist Church

Caddie Dorsey Coleman
Mar. 20, 1871
Feb. 5, 1951
[Moved from Collins Family cemetery at
"Hickory Grove" near Penola, Va.]

SEAMAN
Hervey J. Seaman
Nov. 15, 1860 - Dec. 1933
Raymond R. McWhirt
Mar. 24, 1897 - June 26, 1951
Anna E. Seaman
Jan. 24, 1858 - Apr. 18, 1925
John P. Seaman
June 16, 1857 - Nov. 14, 1926
Charles H. Seaman
Sept. 22, 1865 - Mar. 15, 1944
Eleanor S. McWhirt
Oct. 2, 1890 - Aug. 4, 1957

Raymond R. McWhirt
Virginia
Pvt. Btry. E, 34 Arty. C.A.C.
World War I
March 24, 1897 - June 26, 1951

BLANTON
Robert A.
July 20, 1847 - July 29, 1919
S. Emma
Jan. 20, 1855 - Oct. 10, 1937

Harvey J. Durrett
Oct. 18, 1881
Nov. 12, 1956

Mary E. Blanton
wife of Harvey J. Durrett
July 30, 1891 - April 23, 1934

Charles W. Blanton
Aug. 14, 1891
June 2, 1960

BLANTON
Wm. Lawrence
Nov. 19, 1844 - Nov. 16, 1922
Mattie Winn, His Wife
June 22, 1846 - Dec. 13, 1922

BLANTON
Emmett T.
June 12, 1880 - Jan. 5, 1947
Grace Blanton
June 18, 1888 -

Louis Edward Hockaday, Jr.
Sept. 2, 1952 - July 30, 1958
Budded on earth to bloom in heaven.

HOCKADAY
Hervey S.
Feb. 5, 1902 -
Olive C.
Nov. 27, 1900 - Jan. 14, 1958

CRITTENDEN
T. Maxwell
Feb. 23, 1876 - July 22, 1957
Emma Evans
Jan. 14, 1882 -

Dana H. Garland
Oct. 13, 1913
May 7, 1935

Daughter
June Marie Hicks
June 26, 1940
June 26, 1940

Ruby Garland
April 1939
Jan. 1944

Jeffrey L. Garland
Mar. 15, 1959
Dec. 10, 1959

Olliph C. Carneal
July 22, 1885
March 23, 1923
At Rest.
By His Wife

7

PRINCE
Father
James Pearly
1871-1935
Mother
Anna Lee
1881-1921

STANLEY
A. Walter
Jan. 29, 1860 - Dec. 18, 1924
Annie E.
June 22, 1867 - Sept. 19, 1915
[hand made stone]

Son
John Robert Coleman
Mar. 23, 1915
Jan. 25, 1917

Catherine A. Phillips
Feb. 18, 1850
Oct. 18, 1930
[2-ft. high iron pipe around grave]

HOCKADAY
Henry L.
Oct. 31, 1896 - Dec. 23, 1915
Charlie L.
Dec. 18, 1866 - Apr. 10, 1918
Almedia F.
May 1, 1875 -

Charlie L. Hockaday, Jr.
July 12, 1894
Aug. 12, 1956

Carl Clyde Madison
Oct. 12, 1912
Sept. 8, 1957

In Memory of
S.B. Goodloe
Born July 20, 1862
Died May 2, 1896

Reubena C. Goodloe
1844-1928

COGHILL
Joseph D.
Oct. 4, 1848 - Jan. 10, 1929
Rena C.
Dec. 25, 1851 - Dec. 12, 1918

Mary B. Coghill
1804-1900

DURRETT
Elliott V.
1834-1909
Mary A.
1840-1906

Children of
M. Laf., Jr. & C.M. Young
Elizabeth Blanton
July 28, 1909 - Mar. 9, 1911
Ruth Webster
Oct. 28, 1915 - Dec. 24, 1920

Caroline Virginia Young
Born Aug. 20, 1837
Died Oct. 10, 1916

Marquis Lafayette Young
Born Dec. 22, 1839
Died Feb. 10, 1912

To the Memory of
W.S. Flippo
Born December 24, 1832
Died October 11, 1892

Broken Stone Without Inscription

Eugene Hockaday
Dec. 1903
Aug. 1904

Leanora Hart Hockaday
Sept. 11, 1867
Apr. 11, 1904

Thomas N. Welch
Died Nov. 27, 1908
Age 88 years

Bethany Baptist Church

Lucy Dew Welch
Died Dec. 27, 1910
Age 76 years

BLACKLEY
Willie H.
July 15, 1863 - Jan. 5, 1919
A. Lissie
Oct. 9, 1878 - Sept. 13, 1941

Cyrenus Gallinger
Born Elizabeth, Ontario
Nov. 1, 1840
Died
Oct. 8, 1909
Annamelia Stevenson
wife of C. Gallinger
Born Hinsdale, N.Y.
Sept. 1, 1840
Died Feb. 14, 1906
Edith May Oliver
Born Deerfield, Michigan
May 6, 1869
Died Aug. 15, 1894

Located about 5 miles west of Bowling Green at Paige, Virginia, at the fork of County routes 605 and 638. This church was organized in 1800 by members who left Liberty Baptist Church over the subject of temperance. Reverend Andrew Broaddus I served as its first pastor. Minutes of the Goshen Association of 1802 refer to compulsory tithing which members later objected to and which was ultimately defeated. The present building was erected in 1858, and the oldest marked burial is from 1882.

In describing this congregation, Robert B. Semple in his book, A History of the Rise and Progress of the Baptists in Virginia in 1894, wrote: *Their meetings are solemn without austerity, and lively without any mixture of enthusiasm; their hospitality cordial without parade, and their manners simple and easy without affection. They love without dissimulation, and therefore often meet, not only publicly, but from house to house, for social prayer and conversation.*

Confederate soldiers camped here during the Civil War. In a letter written on May 15, 1863, by John Hampton Chamberlayne, a Confederate soldier, he described the setting of the church: *This is a beautiful country; Bethel Church is about 5 miles from Milford and from Guiney's West of the R.R. on the heights overlooking a beautiful and rich valley of the Mattaponi.*

This site was visited on September 23, 1961.

Sym. Goodloe Coghill
Dec. 27, 1847 - Jan. 21, 1936

Florence Adair
beloved wife of S.G. Coghill
Sept. 25, 1856 - Jul. 11, 1914

Fannie Ellen Coghill
Apr. 25, 1859 - Nov. 17, 1943
daughter of Samuel Hugh Elliott
and Rebekah Dillard Campbell

Aubrey Denton Pickett
Virginia Pvt. Co. K 166 Inf. Regt.
W.W. I, P.H.
Feb. 5, 1895 - Jul. 23, 1957

Aubrey Denton Pickett
Feb. 5, 1895 - July 23, 1957

Ruth May Pickett
Oct. 22, 1927 - Feb. 16, 1937

Pickett Stone Without Inscription

5 Unmarked Graves

James W. Short
Apr. 30, 1920 - May 23, 1945

Benjamin F. Pickett
1856-1920

William Franklin Pugh
Mar. 1, 1886 - Jan. 28, 1887

Mattie V. Pickett
Oct. 17, 1869 - Apr. 27, 1943

Grandfather
Harry Gayle
1883-1906

Grandmother
Ella Gayle
1854-1928

Bethel Baptist Church

Mother
Dorothy G. Mills
1876-1946

Brother
Leslie Lee Mills
Feb. 13, 1904 - Dec. 30, 1908

Father
Edward L. Mills
1869-1953

Sister Geneva Mills
Feb. 2, 1911 - Feb. 2, 1911
[Original Stone Replaced]

MILLS
Dorothy G.
1876-1946
Edward Lee
1869-1953
Their Children
Leslie Lee
1904-1908
Genevieve
1911-1911

Two Illegible Funeral Home Markers

John W. Brown
Serg. 47 Va. Inf.
Confederate States Army
Mar. 17, 1843 - Jan. 30, 1915

Clara B. Long
Died June 28, 1921
Age 30 years.

Emma G. Gayle
Nov. 6, 1954
Age 55 yrs.

GREENSTREET
Sarah S.
1868-1941
Ruben P.
1862-1943

[illegible]
Mar. 1945
90 yrs. old

[illegible]
Lillie W. Shelton
July 28, 1884 - Mar. 31, 1915

Jimmie F. Saunders
Oct. 4, 1909 - Jan. 19, 1946
His wife
Blanche B.
His brother
Walter W.

Blanche B. Saunders
Died Apr. 29, 1957
Age 47 yrs. 11 mos.

Two Unmarked Saunders Family Graves

George Gordon Madison
Died Sept. 1958
Age 52

Richard M. Shelton
Mar. 28, 1897 - Dec. 14, 1956

Unmarked Grave

Jane Shelton
Feb. 14, 1860 - May 12, 1935

Eugene Shelton
Dec. 25, 1882 - Jun. 25, 1953

Lillie W. Shelton
July 28, 1884 - Mar. 31, 1915

Two Illegible Funeral Home Markers

Lorenzo D. Snell
Dec. 10, 1864 - Aug. 5, 1916

Bettie Thomas Snell Vaughan
Died Jan. 10, 1953
Age 81 yrs.

Bethel Baptist Church

Sophia H. Davis
wife of Peter Ramace
Oct. 26, 1816 - Oct. 18, 1906

Porter T. Lyon
Dec. 25, 1829 - Mar. 31, 1913

Nancy Davis
wife of T.P. Lyon
1827-1927

Addie Bigue
Mar. 31, 1856 - Aug. 26, 1902

David Bigue
Mar. 26, 1846 - Jun. 8, 1912

John H. Parr
1842-1897

Virginia Parr
1850-1918

Ada Estelle Parr
wife of Dana C. Smith
Jun. 12, 1883 - Oct. 16, 1918

Maggie Collins Smith
dau. of Dana C. Smith & Ada Parr Smith
Sept. 30, 1915 - Oct. 19, 1918

Maggie C. Parr
1842-1925

John Parr
1906-1892

Carlton Woolfolk
1878-1889

Fannie A. Woolfolk
1851-1896

W.A. Woolfolk
1849-1920

E.J. Stevens
1822-1882

Bettie White Stevens
Apr. 10, 1837 - Apr. 10, 1910

Benjamin F. Mills
Pvt. Co. K, 47 Va. Inf.
Confederate States Army
1841-1899

Charlie Mills
1867-1886

Columbia G. Mills
1845-1917

Jessie C. Vaughan
Virginia
Pvt. Co. L, 116 Infantry
World War I
Mar. 6, 1894 - Jan. 1, 1958

CARTER
Asby
Aug. 10, 1902 - Nov. 15, 1943
Eva
Aug. 1, 1892 - June 15, 1966
[handmade marker]

12

This church is located 14.8 miles south of Bowling Green, Virginia, on U.S. Route 2, and 1.4 miles east on Route 30. Bethel Methodist Church was organized in 1854. The original building is of rectangular brick laid in the common bond pattern. As was typical of churches of that period, there is a small balcony to the rear of the building.

At the back of the sanctuary there are two memorial windows, one erected in memory of Thomas Price Jackson (1806-1880), and the other to Robert Sale Peatross (1805-1880), who were founders of the church.

The oldest marker found bears the date 1904. Visited on December 26, 1961.

Edwin Price Beazley
July 11, 1871 - Aug. 27, 1941

Evelyn S. Beazley
Dec. 16, 1875 - Apr. 6, 1916

Archibald Samuel
May 2, 1843 - Nov. 7, 1904

Mary C. Samuel
Apr. 1, 1842 - Dec. 30, 1907

Nannie Tunstall
Sept. 14, 1839 - Apr. 8, 1910

Robert Asbury Gibson
Nov. 10, 1916 - Dec. 8, 1916
Helen Katherine Gibson
May 10, 1918 - Aug. 6, 1918

Robbie M. Gibson
Jan. 26, 1899 - Jul. 9, 1909

Robert Asbury Gibson
Nov. 10, 1916 - Dec. 8, 1916
Helen Katherine Gibson
May 10, 1918 - August 6, 1918

Richard V. Owen
May 20, 1882 - Jul. 3, 1943

Martha E. Owen
Aug. 12, 1886 - Jul. 10, 1948

Infant

SOUTHWORTH
Arra Lee R.
March 15, 1876 - Dec. 17, 1948
Charles W.
March 12, 1863 - Sept. 1, 1920

Andrew J. Bennett
1836-1912

Caroline T. Bennett
1839-1915

Seth Rosson
March 1, 1852
March 8, 1921

Our Mother
S.A. Rosson
Aug. 13, 1852 - Jun. 26, 1916

Robert Stanley Rosson
Jan. 14, 1883 - May 12, 1947

Clifford Linwood Rosson
Oct. 18, 1891 - Nov. 11, 1954

A.D. Poppieton

Mary L. Poppieton

Bethel Methodist Church

Elizabeth Southworth
Apr. 5, 1907 - Apr. 7, 1907

Richard M. Turner
1913-1937

TURNER
Samuel F.
1905-1909
Pearl V.
1907-1909

Fannie Turner Mundie
1908-1934

Mother
Bettie B. Turner
Mar. 19, 1875 - Jun. 29, 1941

Father
William H. Turner
May 11, 1870 - Jun. 4, 1944

Lloyd T. Taylor
Nov. 10, 1905 - Nov. 12, 1920

Thomas Earl Taylor
Aug. 26, 1876 - Feb. 14, 1952
Annie Bell Taylor
Jan. 30, 1882 - Jul. 31, 1951

Alma Maude
daughter of W.H. & J.B. Blanton
Dec. 4, 1922 - Nov. 18, 1923

William Harold Blanton
April 10, 1894 - March 9, 1935

Gladys Southworth Taylor
Oct. 6, 1902 - Dec. 15, 1948

Lewis Southworth
Nov. 24, 1868 - Dec. 11, 1919

Infant son of Eva Turner
and Robert S. Hughes
May 22, 1927

Daughter of
Odel and Goldie
Southworth

Leroy Turner
Died Nov. 3, 1953
Age 78 yrs.

Jennie Toler Turner
Died Oct. 14, 1951
Age 78 yrs.

J. Arthur Moren
Jul. 7, 1883 - Sept. 29, 1959

Alma T. Moren
Aug. 20, 1880 - Nov. 24, 1945

James T. Toler
Jul. 20, 1876 - Jan. 12, 1944

Ella Kelley
wife of James R. Toler
1876-1922

V. Katherine Seal
infant daughter of L.F. & V.L. Seal
Aug. 19, 1927 - Aug. 19, 1927

Mother
Bettie Vaughan Samuel
Mar. 12, 1844 - Mar. 4, 1923
Father
Eugene Samuel
May 1, 1844 - Mar. 10, 1923

S. Dudley Mitchell
March 27, 1904 - January 6, 1930

Everett W. Mitchell
Jul. 1, 1906 - Apr. 23, 1942

Victoria S. Mitchell
Oct. 15, 1877 - Jul. 21, 1949

Joseph L. Mitchell
Oct. 8, 1874 - Oct. 22, 1956

Bert R. Anderson
Feb. 23, 1872 - Nov. 17, 1947

Bethel Methodist Church

Isaac S. Cooper
Mar. 8, 1878 - Nov. 26, 1948

Two Unmarked Graves

Arthur R. Kelly
1883-1958

Emmett A. Kelly
1923-1924

Unmarked Grave

Robert S. Hughes
Virginia
PFC Hq. Co. 318 Inf. 80 Div.
World War I
Apr. 25, 1891 - May 28, 1948

Deliah Southard Hughes
July 20, 1867 - Oct. 23, 1929

Henry Ernest Hughes
March 27, 1896 - August 26, 1932

Henry Peyton Hughes
Apr. 16, 1865 - June 12, 1951

Infant Son of A.L. & M.M. Moren
Feb. 11, 1941

Infant daughter of J.L. & L.B. Mitchell
Jan. 4, 1941

Arlene
daughter of C.L. & P.B. Mitchell
Oct. 6, 1933 - Nov. 1, 1933

Infant son of C.L. & P.B. Mitchell
Jan. 2, 1936

Elijah A. Mitchell
Oct. 28, 1876 - Oct. 10, 1950

Sarah S. Mitchell
Sept. 10, 1879 - Oct. 9, 1955

Iron Basket Monument

Section Across the Road

Infant son of
C.H. & Lottie M. Johnson
May 28, 1924

Four Unmarked Graves

Charles Herman Johnson
June 16, 1896 - May 14, 1957

Lottie Mitchell Johnson
June 3, 1898 - Dec. 5, 1932

JOHNSON
Mary Callie
1872-1956
wife of
William T.
1860-1917

Two Cement Slabs

Audrey Lillian Johnson
Infant Daughter of
Lucy & Burnley Johnson
d. June 18, 1930

W. Earl Johnson
1903-1923

15

St. Asaph's Episcopal Church (c.1832), Now Bowling Green Methodist Church

Bowling Green Methodist Church

Located on the west side of Main Street, just south of Milford Street, in Bowling Green, Virginia. The church was organized in 1832 as an Episcopal Church. The original church, which was rectangular in shape and built of brick, is today enclosed in the middle of the present structure. Additions were made to the building in the 1940's, using materials salvaged from old Upper Zion Baptist Church when it was town down to make way for Camp A.P. Hill.

Originally there were many graves behind this church, but when the landscaping was done recently, these graves were levelled over and there were only two or three mounds left which were still visable in 1937.

Membership of the Episcopal Church, originally on this site, became so small by 1866 that its members transferred to St. Margaret's Episcopal Church, near Ruther Glen. At that time, the building was sold to the Methodists with the consent of the Bishop of the Diocese. The Methodists began here in 1866 under the leadership of Rev. John G. Rowe who lies buried in back of the church. Rev. Rowe earlier in life was a Baptist minister, later converting to Methodism. A tablet to his memory was placed inside the church.

This site was visited on April 27, 1963.

Rev. John Gallatin Rowe
February 27, 1827 - April 16, 1891

Emma, wife of Edgar Rowe
February 24, 1847 - August 23, 1884

Maggie Wilson
daughter of J.S. & Mary Davis
November 10, 1858 - November 11, 1879

Laura Jackson
daughter of Joseph S. & Mary Davis
December 1, 1865 - October 26, 1867

Mattie G.
daughter of R.D. & S.E. Arnall
June 18, 1865 - October 26, 1887

Carmel Baptist Church

The church is located 12 miles southwest of Bowling Green, Virginia, on U.S. Route 1, near the intersection of State Route 207 and County Route 654. Carmel Baptist Church was organized as Mt. Carmel, and earlier known as Burruss's Church. The original site was south of the present one, and took its name from its first pastor Reverend Burruss.

The first house of worship was erected in 1773. The congregation moved to the present site in 1838. That building burned in 1874. When the present structure was built, the name was changed from Burruss' Church to Mt. Carmel. Later the "Mt." was dropped. This church has the distinction of being the oldest church in continuous service in Caroline County. Most of the tombstones are from the 20th century, with the oldest on being from 1888.

Visited on December 26, 1961.

Fleming T. Bibb
Oct. 5, 1852 - Apr. 7, 1914

Maggie C. Smith (Bibb)
1852 - Dec. 19, 1925
Harry Clevinger Bibb
1884 - May 8, 1959

John V. Wright
Dec. 9, 1854 - Feb. 16, 1931

Fannie Bibb Wright
Jul. 23, 1856 - Jul. 1953

Sophie H. Bibb
Apr. 8, 1854 - Apr. 16, 1938

Charles L. Coffey
Jul. 31, 1868 - June 21, 1940
Alice H. Coffey
Jan. 27, 1872 - Feb. 27, 1960

Dewey Coffey
Feb. 5, 1899 - Jan. 7, 1919

Lloyd W. Coffey
Dec. 21, 1893 - Sept. 7, 1959
Mattie M. Coffey
Dec. 19, 1894 -

Doris Lorene Middlebrook
Sept. 21, 1928 - Oct. 7, 1928

A. Vernon
son of M.E. & S.W. Middlebrook
Dec. 16, 1908 - Sept. 7, 1917

Sicilian W. Middlebrook
Mar. 28, 1874 - Mar. 2, 1956
Mary Carter Middlebrook
May 28, 1876 - Apr. 23, 1934

Cornelius T. Middlebrook
Aug. 12, 1864 - Dec. 12, 1937

Rosa Y. Middlebrook
Apr. 22, 1871 - Sept. 4, 1946

Dorothy Elizabeth
Dec. 4, 1947 - Dec. 22, 1947

Mary Ellen
Dec. 4, 1947 - Dec. 24, 1947

Catherine R. Kennon
Died Oct. 11, 1921
Aged 63 yrs.

J. Franklin Hutcherson
Jan. 6, 1894 - Feb. 23, 1961

18

Carmel Baptist Church

Leanious C. Middlebrook
1867-1925
Catherine D. Middlebrook
1880-1951
Clarence L. Middlebrook
1921-1923

Clarence L. Goodwin
May 4, 1885 - Feb. 25, 1930

Harold P. Goodwin
Dec. 24, 1917 - Oct. 18, 1918

S.L. Smith
Apr. 24, 1840 - Aug. 31, 1924

Virginia Smith
Jan. 1, 1864 - Jul. 28, 1937

Bessie R. Brown
June 17, 1889 - Oct. 7, 1954

Charles W. Brown
May 7, 1872 - Mar. 12, 1945

Allie Sacra
Virginia
Pvt. U.S. Marine Corps
World War I
Mar. 6, 1895 - Nov. 4, 1960

James L. Collison
Apr. 26, 1930 - Jul. 10, 1930

Bettie B. Schwalbe
1875-1951
Otto G. Schwalbe
1872-1938

Ernestina
wife of O.G. Schwalbe
Oct. 20, 1867 - May 8, 1917

Samuel J. Walser
1877-1959

Fannie N. Duffey
1902-1959

Frank Jr.
son of Frank & Nellie McAllister
Nov. 12, 1938 - Apr. 18, 1939

Unmarked Grave

Lewis Walter Middlebrook
Apr. 19, 1869 -
Willie Cannon Middlebrook
July 10, 1871 - May 15, 1930

Funeral Marker

Unmarked Cement Slab

Raleigh Ira Smith
Jan. 31, 1876 - Apr. 9, 1950
Salome Quarles Smith
Jan. 29, 1875 - Jul. 20, 1960

Judson W. Smith
Jun. 30, 1879 - Jul. 10, 1954

Infant son of J.W. & E.H. Smith
May 14, 1919

Maurice C. Smith
Nov. 29, 1917 - Jul. 18, 1935

Clarence E. Smith
Jun. 25, 1914 - Apr. 28, 1943

Nannie Houston Nelson
Dec. 14, 1861 - Jan. 11, 1940

James B. Trevillian
May 19, 1859 - May 15, 1937
Rennie H. Trevillian
Jan. 12, 1864 - Jan. 21, 1941

Otho W. Southworth
Jul. 14, 1858 - Jul. 10, 1921

Minnie Trevellian
wife of O.W. Southworth
Apr. 27, 1856 - Jan. 10, 1927

C.R. Cannon
Died Nov. 24, 1947

19

Carmel Baptist Church

Arch F. Cannon
1845-1928

Lewis F. Jones
Feb. 27, 1866 - Dec. 26, 1949
Mary C. Jones
Mar. 29, 1876 - Jul. 23, 1951

Charles S. Madison
Mar. 21, 1890 - Jan. 22, 1937

Cary J. Patterson
Apr. 11, 1877 - Feb. 28, 1941

Abi C. Patterson
Aug. 11, 1886 - Mar. 6, 1956

Unmarked Grave

Vernon L. Patterson
Dec. 21, 1901 - Feb. 8, 1929

Josephine B. Patterson
Oct. 11, 1878 - June 3, 1948

James L. Patterson
Virginia
Sgt. 4 Artillery
SP AM War
June 13, 1875 - Oct. 7, 1950

Jennie P. Smith
Jul. 31, 1875 - May 29, 1944

Hattie T. Smith
wife of R.S. Smith
Feb. 3, 1844 - Dec. 28, 1915

Robert S. Smith
Nov. 18, 1843 - Apr. 11, 1922

Charles S. Smith
Feb. 22, 1878 - Aug. 8, 1938

Father
J. Campbell Smith
Mar. 16, 1888 - Dec. 26, 1916

Son
Wilson W. Smith
Jul. 12, 1915 - Dec. 27, 1916

T. Marshall Smith
Jul. 12, 1915 - Mar. 7, 1921

Myrtle Wright Smith
Jan. 1, 1857 - Mar. 20, 1932

V. Josephine Smith
Died Mar. 18, 1923
Age 86

Nellie H. Haley
May 5, 1886 - Nov. 20, 1919

Jesse C. Haley
Apr. 17, 1883 - Dec. 26, 1954

Maude H. Blanton
Feb. 27, 1869 - Nov. 26, 1952

Robert L. Blanton
Mar. 6, 1869 - Sept. 13, 1955

G.S. Hargrave
May 11, 1867 - Jan. 12, 1940

Annie K. Burruss
Dec. 16, 1866 - Dec. 13, 1957

Edwin E. Burruss
Oct. 14, 1865 - Mar. 18, 1932

Infant son of Mr. & Mrs. R.B. Houston
Nov. 22, 1940

Joseph Ryland Houston
Dec. 22, 1872 - Feb. 15, 1956

Argyle James Haley
Apr. 17, 1879 - May 19, 1930

Two Unmarked Graves

Sadie H. Flagg
Sept. 16, 1871 - Dec. 19, 1940
E. Fletcher Flagg
Nov. 20, 1870 -

Carmel Baptist Church

Funeral Marker

Roderick D. Flagg
1899-1937

Annie Welford Hill
Aug. 1866 - May 1950

James R. Blanton
May 7, 1894 - Dec. 28, 1912
Carrie Lee Blanton
Nov. 10, 1892 - Nov. 19, 1955
James R. Blanton
Feb. 15, 1864 - Feb. 7, 1921
Cora L. Blanton
Jun. 28, 1864 - Aug. 27, 1937
Mary Louise Blanton
Jun. 9, 1900 - Jul. 26, 1957
Clarice R. Blanton
Mar. 14, 1887 - Aug. 4, 1888
M. Evelyn Blanton
May 27, 1889 - Dec. 30, 1893

Sallie W. Hargrave
Oct. 4, 1867 - Oct. 16, 1943

Douglas Coleman
Dec. 27, 1873 - May 21, 1950

Lucy H. Coleman
Aug. 19, 1873 - Sept. 14, 1955

James Hayes (Father)
May 13, 1877 - Oct. 11, 1941
Sarah A. Hayes (Mother)
Mar. 10, 1878 - Nov. 14, 1950

Kenneth Hayes (Father)
Jul. 23, 1908 - Feb. 10, 1944
Louise S. Hayes
Aug. 17, 1910 -

George W. Stevenson
1881-1944

Our beloved son
James Patrick Terry
1930-1946

Ella Terry Blanton
Died 1942
Patrick H. Terry
Aug. 5, 1863 - Feb. 16, 1947
Millie J. Terry
Oct. 6, 1873 - Jul. 22, 1952

Daughter
Myrtle Terry Carter
1913-1943

Ernest P. Campbell
1876-1956
Ella G. Campbell
1890-

Mother
Maude Claytor Smith
May 24, 1890 - Mar. 13, 1919

Husband
Ervin E. Smith
May 12, 1886 - Nov. 5, 1949

Bessie Staples Smith
May 27, 1889 - Nov. 2, 1954

Pembleton B. Smith
Oct. 20, 1900 - Dec. 31, 1957

Ellen Roy Smith
Aug. 23, 1908 - Oct. 2, 1941

Infant Baby

Robert Lee Jones
May 1, 1895 - Feb. 18, 1939

Cornelius Linden Allen
Apr. 6, 1938
Vera Coleman Allen
Oct. 12, 1879 - Sept. 10, 1956

Ernest England
1879-1935

G.E. England
1872-1945

Carmel Baptist Church

Grace E. Merchant
1872-1945

Pattie M. England
1878-1958

Mary McConnell England
1880-1958

Maude E. England
1870-1958

Lillard A. Thomas
Virginia
Pvt. Hq. Btry. 6 Field Arty.
Jan. 24, 1905 - Dec. 19, 1960

Infant daughter of Robert & Martha Parr
May 25, 1938

Infant son of R.E. & Rebecca Wright
Mar. 31, 1944

Estelle Walton Smith Quarles
May 21, 1877 - June 13, 1952

Baby Boy Peatross
Mar. 2, 1928 - Mar. 4, 1928

Rufus Page Carter
Mar. 14, 1862 - Sept. 8, 1928
In Memory of His Wife
Myrtle Donahoe Carter
Mar. 18, 1866 - Nov. 12, 1895
Buried in Family Cemetery Elsewhere in Caroline County

F. Zollicoffer Peatross
May 30, 1868 - Mar. 13, 1930

Mother
Lannie A. Cobb
Feb. 9, 1860 - Oct. 8, 1925

Lloyd Cobb, son of A.L. & E.C. Cobb
Nov. 24, 1900 - Nov. 13, 1919

Audie L. Smith
Sept. 11, 1875 - Nov. 12, 1923

George Wilson Quarles
Dec. 5, 1847 - Mar. 4, 1934

In Memory of the following members of the QUARLES Family who were buried in graveyards at the sites of "Moss Side" and "Jerusalem," one-time QUARLES Homes on the North Anna River about 2½ miles S.E. of this memorial:

--

Wm. QUARLES, d. 1817 & his wife
Mary TERRY, their sons:
Minor QUARLES, 1762-1831 and
wife Sarah NELSON
Wilson QUARLES, 1783-1831 and
wife Mary S. HACKETT
Nancy QUARLES, 1797-1830,
dau. of Minor
Peter QUARLES, 1797-1859,
son of Minor
William Thomas, 1818-1907,
son of Wilson
his wives:
Mary Ellen REDD, d. 1849
Annie M. SMITH, 1825-1851
Marcella ROGANNI, 1841-1909
Thomas E. CHANDLER, 1860-1895,
husb. of Lillian C. Quarles, dau. of
William Thomas

Mollie G. Hackett
June 19, 1846 - Jul. 24, 1929

William B. Smith
Jul. 4, 1885 - Nov. 7, 1944

Lennie B. Smith
Jan. 3, 1891 - Jan. 11, 1942

Carl E. Smith
Oct. 8, 1884 - Jan. 27, 1941
Ivy W. Smith
Jan. 17, 1885 -

Richard F. Taylor
Sept. 22, 1904 - Mar. 16, 1956

Farley Bullock
wife of Gregory Smith
1890-1931

22

Carmel Baptist Church

Patricia Ann
daughter of G.P. & E.S. Smith
Sept. 1933 - Dec. 1940

Charles Dudley Brothers
1930-1950

J. Eddie Wright
Jan. 23, 1867 - Apr. 13, 1933
Mattie H. Wright
Oct. 28, 1861 - Apr. 16, 1938

Emmer L. Terry
Apr. 9, 1882 - Jan. 8, 1946
James A. Terry
Jan. 4, 1872 - Mar. 18, 1944

Four Unmarked Graves

Sidney E. Carneal
Jan. 20, 1872 - June 28, 1942

Sarah Long Carneal
Oct. 4, 1873 - Jan. 10, 1945

William Conway Jones
PFC
3347 QM Truck Co.
World War II
Oct. 20, 1911 - Jan. 29, 1960

Albert H. Cecil
May 19, 1876 - Oct. 7, 1959
Mattie M. Cecil
Feb. 10, 1882 -

William Henry Yarbrough
Nov. 15, 1916 - Oct. 2, 1937

James John Yarbrough
June 10, 1868 - May 27, 1950

Harriet Gentry Yarbrough
Aug. 1, 1875 - June 28, 1954

Lewis L. Yarbrough
May 10, 1905 - Oct. 19, 1959

Mother
B.L. Pickett
1902-1937

E.C. Pickett
1937-1942

Grave With Angel Monument

Unmarked Grave

Elsie Oneal
daughter of G.J. and J.R. Jones
Sept. 20, 1925 - Nov. 8, 1932

Edward Lewis Carneal
Sept. 25, 1928 - June 7, 1931

Hilda A. Carneal
Feb. 20, 1935 - Dec. 23, 1937

My Mother
Sarah Yarbrough
Feb. 10, 1864 - Jul. 28, 1939

My Father
Henry Yarbrough
Nov. 10, 1863 - May 2, 1943

Two Unmarked Graves

Herbert H. Tate
June 18, 1882 - Jan. 8, 1957

Jeff Taylor
Mar. 28, 1863 - Mar. 25, 1936
Ella G. Taylor
Jan. 28, 1868 - Apr. 22, 1929

Lelia Taylor
Nov. 22, 1896 - Mar. 13, 1960

Robert Avon Peatross
Sept. 12, 1914 -
Helen Mildred Peatross
May 26, 1918 - May 18, 1957

Christine Blanton Wright
Jan. 27, 1902 - Dec. 28, 1949

Carmel Baptist Church

Florence T. Spencer
Jan. 1, 1892 -
Joseph E. Spencer
Aug. 12, 1885 - Dec. 23, 1949

Unmarked Grave

Pleasant B. Coghill
Feb. 5, 1896 - Aug. 24, 1953
Isla Sale Coghill
May 30, 1894 - May 6, 1958

Ruby Willey
Died 1959

Infant daughter of
Helen M. and Ezell E. Nelson
Dec. 6, 1946 - Dec. 6, 1946

Charlie Collison
Jul. 9, 1890 - Mar. 29, 1958
Hattie J. Collison
May 7, 1889 -

Mary E. Caruthers
May 22, 1961 - May 22, 1961

Clifton Hudgens
West Virginia
Pvt. Co. C, 304 Field Sig. Bn.
World War I
Mar. 18, 1895 - Sept. 18, 1959

George M. Tate
June 20, 1920 - Dec. 27, 1955

P.F.C. Herbert L. Tate
Hq. & Hq. Co. 1st Abn. B.G.
502nd Inf.
July 29, 1940 - Dec. 15, 1959

Skeeter
Steven Wayne Dean
Dec. 17, 1946 - Aug. 26, 1955

Dickerson Sons
Born - Died Mar. 1952

Irene Terry Sanford
1920-1948

Mrs. Lula Prince Gayle
Died Jul. 30, 1961
Age 76

Wife
Jessie Vandermark Dudley
1912-1954

Edward Thomas Jones, Jr.
Died Apr. 9, 1961
Age 32

Edward T. Jones
1886-1954
Susie M. Jones
1897-19

Oliver G. Coates
Dec. 21, 1879 - Aug. 25, 1948

Unmarked Grave

Richard Madison
Aug. 31, 1872 - Nov. 1, 1955

Annie P. Madison
Aug. 3, 1890 - Apr. 12, 1961

Two Unmarked Graves

Annie Middlebrooks
1895-1955

Joe M. Collison
Virginia
P.F.C. 119 Inf.
World War II P.H.
Jul. 1, 1909 - Jul. 29, 1944

Willie M. Collison
Died Nov. 11, _____
Age 70 yrs.

S.F. Holloway
5.7.1850 - 11.1.1925

24

Site of Old Carmel Baptist Church

The church at this site burned in 1836, and the congregation moved north. Located .4 mile south of Carmel Church, Virginia, on Route 1. Turn left at the south entrance to Tick Tock Inn and go into the woods about 100 years. The cemetery is enclosed in a wire fence, and covers about 1/4 acre. It is overgrown in honeysuckle, periwinkle, bob grass, and large cedar trees. There is evidence of many graves, but only a few are marked. The tops of some tombstones have been broken off and cannot now be found. This site was visited on April 24, 1963.

C. Mills Madison
September 23, 1944
age 21 years

Nannie T. Madison
March 1, 1881 - January 1, 1913

Wife of J.K.P. Middlebrook
August 20, 1912, age 84 years

Rennie J. Jones
April 24, 1897 - August 4, 1920

Concord Baptist Church

Concord Baptist Church

Located near Dawn, Virginia, 14.9 miles south of Bowling Green on U.S. Route 2, and 1 mile northwest on Route 651. This congregation was organized on July 1, 1841. The original building was located across the road from the present one, and was erected with funds provided by Joseph Brame who also donated the land for the site. In 1857, the building was replaced and the original site became the church cemetery. The 1857 structure is white stucco over brick. In recent years, additions have been made to the building.

The congregation for Concord Baptist Church came largely from Reed's Baptist Church. When the church was first organized, there were 74 white members and 12 black members. By 1859, the congregation had grown to 86 white members and 262 black members. The constitution of the church stated that the government of the church would remain in the hands of the free white males which probably kept it from becoming strictly a black church after the Civil War.

Visited on September 23, 1961.

James Preston Campbell
October 24, 1874 - April 21, 1953

Louise Terrell Campbell
December 10, 1888-September 17, 1961

Sherwood C. Bowers
July 30, 1876 - Nov. 14, 1943

Margaret Pollard Bowers
Apr. 7, 1885 - Jan. 9, 1961

Mordecai W. Andrews
July 7, 1896 - Mar. 30, 1948

Georgia H. Andrews
Dec. 23, 1877 - Sept. 30, 1942

Elizabeth M. Long
May 17, 1878 - Feb. 4, 1960

Mary Davis Long
Oct. 6, 1915 - Sept. 17, 1948

George S. Morrison
Mar. 27, 1869 - Dec. 19, 1942

Annie H. Morrison
May 27, 1876 - Feb. 21, 1942

Alfred Hill Morrison
Virginia
Lt. Col., U.S. Army
World War II Korea Cr.
Dec. 24, 1909 - Jun. 11, 1957

Infant Son of
Thomas & Waverly Burruss
[Died] April [29,] 1957
[Age 1 day]

Emma Burruss Jeter
Apr. 6, 1899
Jan. 3, 1959
Age 58

J.P. Thomas
1877-1942

Unmarked Grave

Cornelius S. Southworth
Mar. 26, 1873 - Jun. 30, 1926

27

Concord Baptist Church

Douglas P. Southworth
Sept. 13, 1924 - Aug. 29, 1941

George W. Kelley
May 1, 1876 - Feb. 2, 1957

My Wife
Ella Kelley
June 14, 1885 - Feb. 24, 1942

Ida V. Kelley
July 18, 1887 - Sept. 12, 1959
My Husband
Mordecai Kelley
May 6, 1877
May 17, 1944

M.L. Barlow
1947-1947

I.W. Barlow
1948-1948

G.E. Barlow
1950-1950

Our Baby
Infant Son
Johnson
1961

John Edward Mitchell
Mar. 29, 1928 - Oct. 18, 1954

Infant son of Mildred and Dewey Simms
Feb. 11, 1949 - Feb. 12, 1949

Ashton Blanton Hart
May 8, 1898 - May 2, 1953

Andrew Beal Ball
Virginia
Cpl. 556 Base Unit AAF
World War II
Oct. 2, 1919 - Feb. 23, 1954

Cecil Clyde Young
May 27, 1903 - Feb. 7, 1957

William Ernest Young
July 8, 1870 - Dec. 13, 1938

Gertrude Blake Young
Sept. 20, 1871 - Dec. 15, 1953

Robert C. Richardson
May 9, 1880 - Oct. 8, 1950

Addie S. Richardson
May 4, 1885 - Mar. 14, 1945

Viola Mae Noel
May 2, 1907 - Oct. 11, 1949

Robert F. Simpkins
Jun. 28, 1885 - Jun. 2, 1944

Thomas Monroe Tribble
Sept. 12, 1881 - Sept. 27, 1943

Burnett Doggett
Oct. 27, 1917 - Feb. 6, 1961

Nannie R. Doggett
Oct. 4, 1924 - Nov. 22, 1948

Robert L. Taylor
Jan. 21, 1871 - Dec. 12, 1943

Eva W. Taylor
Aug. 1, 1878 - Feb. 3, 1949

O.F. Tribble
1880-1951

George H. Grunwell
May 19, 1903 - May 9, 1960

Nina B. Southworth
1880-1958

Robert P. Southworth
Jul. 28, 1916 - Jun. 4, 1954

Henry T. Southworth
Nov. 6, 1907 - Oct. 5, 1930

Bloomy Southworth
Apr. 20, 1882 - Feb. 23, 1923

28

Concord Baptist Church

Florence Hohmann
September 22, 1924
September 30, 1961
[Statue of Jesus]

Dorothy Carneal
Sept. 26, 1901 - Feb. 19, 1944

Walter Carneal
Died Mar. 4, 1940

James C. Southworth
1919-1957

George W. Southworth
Feb. 1, 1880 - Feb. 20, 1956

Sarah J. Satterwhite
Jul. 6, 1870 - Jan. 19, 1945

Enoch L. Satterwhite
June 15, 1865 - Sept. 22, 1936

Chastine Satterwhite
Aug. 7, 1894 - Jan. 6, 1916

Clarence Lee Satterwhite
Apr. 21, 1892 - Oct. 26, 1917

Eula May Satterwhite
Jan. 19, 1907 - Nov. 7, 1917

Lucy Mae Satterwhite
Jan. 17, 1915 - June 2, 1935

SATTERWHITE
William G.
1890-1949
Lizzie L.
1896-

Leonard E. Cannon
Virginia
P.F.C., 689 Ord. Armo.
World War II
Sept. 7, 1908 - Nov. 6, 1958

My Son
Maxie M. Cannon
Jan. 22, 1923 - Sept. 28, 1957

Our Father
Leslie Franklin Cannon
Jul. 26, 1905 - Sept. 5, 1954

Our Son
Alvin Clyde Cannon
Apr. 3, 1911 - Sept. 12, 1953

Our Mother
Bettie Mitchell Cannon
Jun. 25, 1878 - Oct. 14, 1958

Charles A. Cannon
May 13, 1875 - Jun. 15, 1935

Our Father
Charles Preston Cannon
Jul. 10, 1899 - Jan. 31, 1953

William R. Doggett, Sr.
Dec. 15, 1884 - May 19, 1938

Claude B. Doggett
Dec. 4, 1919 - Jan. 21, 1921

Frances L. Doggett
Sept. 4, 1913 - Oct. 14, 1919

Melville W. Andrews
1870-1946

Lilian B. Andrews
1866-1915

ANDREWS

John W. Young
Jul. 29, 1857 - July 16, 1937

Florence B. Young
Sept. 16, 1886 - Nov. 19, 1952

Ella Young Turner
May 13, 1912 - Feb. 18, 1957

Emmett Hunter Hutcheson
Apr. 15, 1876 - Jan. 25, 1959

Mollie Bowers Hutcheson
Aug. 20, 1876 - Mar. 17, 1957

Concord Baptist Church

J.H. Bowers
1868-1940

Thomas Cary Bowers
Oct. 19, 1861 - Aug. 27, 1953

Walter T. Bullock
1889-1953

Rosa L. Bullock
1861-1953

Sidney M. Bullock
1855-1929

Charles Aston Saunders
Feb. 15, 1850 - Aug. 24, 1936

Elizabeth Hill Saunders
Dec. 8, 1856 - Sept. 26, 1928

Nannie W. Shackelford
1849-1927

Arthur Linsey Southworth
husband of Dora L. Southworth
1883-1930

Mother
Mary F. Southworth
June 22, 1853 - Jul. 9, 1929

Father
James N. Southworth
Apr. 3, 1851 - Sept. 23, 1916

Infant son of
Frank & Emma Doggett
1916

Infant son of
Frank & Emma Doggett
1918

Elizabeth Long Doggett
Jul. 18, 1860 - Jul. 5, 1955

Robert Fulton Doggett
Oct. 30, 1855 - May 4, 1925

Harry Doggett
Mar. 13, 1887 - May 28, 1911

James E. Young
Nov. 16, 1876 - Feb. 5, 1954

Percy L. Young
Jun. 18, 1915 - Mar. 28, 1936

Myrtle Young Barlow
Sept. 15, 1899 - Apr. 5, 1918

Harry Alexander Barlow
Dec. 25, 1891 - Jun. 2, 1956

William L. Terrell
1891-1961

Maude W. Long
wife of Wm. L. Terrell
Jan. 26, 1896 - Feb. 11, 1930

Maude Willis
dau. of Wm. L. and M.W. Terrell
Jul. 1, 1924 - Jul. 4, 1928

Clarence W. Barlow
Mar. 1, 1880 - Jan. 24, 1940

Mary E. Barlow
Dec. 20, 1868 - Mar. 23, 1946

John J. Atkinson
Apr. 3, 1842 - Apr. 22, 1922

Eliza J. Atkinson
Jun. 1, 1838 - May 24, 1912

Lewis V. Atkinson
Mar. 22, 1871 - Jan. 5, 1934

Bertha B. Atkinson
Dec. 18, 1884 - Aug. 1, 1954

Edith G. Atkinson
Aug. 11, 1905 - Oct. 2, 1906

John W. Barlow
Nov. 14, 1840 - Feb. 12, 1926

Concord Baptist Church

Nettie E. Barlow
Mar. 13, 1886 - Jan. 29, 1956

Pearl F. Barlow
Sept. 5, 1897 -

V.I. Freeman
1934-1934

Son
Augustus Monroe Freeman
Feb. 25, 1921 - Feb. 10, 1957

Charles E. Young
Mar. 29, 1900 - Dec. 6, 1956

J. Raleigh Barlow
1916-1932

Our Cousin
John Grover Long
May 14, 1919 - Jun. 21, 1942

W. Ruth Long
1892-1941

George L. Long
1883-1940

Unmarked Stone

Marshall Franklin Peatross
Died Apr. 30, 1961
Age 47

Marshall F. Peatross
Virginia
Pvt. 545, A.A. A.W. B.N. C.A.C.
World War II
Jan. 12, 1914 - April 30, 1961

J. James Peatross
Nov. 12, 1879 - Feb. 11, 1941

Harvey C. Wiltshire
Oct. 27, 1881 - Dec. 20, 1926

William S. Bowers
Jul. 26, 1844 - Dec. 5, 1906
Member of 30th Va. Regt.
Corses Brigade Pickett's Div.
[Mason]

Robert H. Bowers
1853-1902

Emily R. Bowers
wife of William S. Bowers
Jan. 16, 1843 - Jul. 15, 1908

Harvie
son of W.S. & E.R. Bowers
Jul. 18, 1869 - Jul. 19, 1889

R.E. Duvall

ATEHBERTON

L.C. Pollard, M.D.
1831-1902

Henry A. Jeter
1905-1960

Mary E. Freeman
1829-1910

James W. Freeman
1814-1897

Elizabeth F. Hill
1859-1907

Robert D. Freeman
1861-1942

Emma D. Freeman
1877-1957

Wallace Emmett Bowers
Feb. 14, 1917 - Nov. 4, 1918

James Ryland Bowers
Apr. 11, 1866 - Jun. 9, 1930

Ann Grimes Lowery
1830-1904

Concord Baptist Church

John Franklin Douglas
Died Jun. 18, 1934

BOWERS
Charles Clifford
May 11, 1870 - Sept. 13, 1943
Mary Chenault
Jan. 23, 1888 -

Fannie E. Wiltshire
wife of John F. Douglas
Died Dec. 17, 1959

Mother
Mary J. Atkins
Died Feb. 13, 1944

Allena Covington
wife of C.H. Schools
Died Aug. 20, 1904

Samuel Lott Chiles
May 30, 1875 - Sept. 1, 1931

John Edmund Chiles
Sept. 5, 1847 - May 30, 1914

Virginia Rosson Chiles
Mar. 21, 1874 - Nov. 2, 1948

George Wilson Chiles
Jan. 4, 1909 - Apr. 19, 1956

C.E. Bowers
Thornton's Btry.
Virginia Infantry
C.S.A.

Unmarked Grave

Our Grandmother
Mary A. Cannon
Sept. 3, 1850 - Jan. 7, 1924

William F. Mitchell
Oct. 7, 1869 - Aug. 16, 1934

Phoebe S. Mitchell
Feb. 27, 1867 - Apr. 2, 1941

Wm. T. Lumpkin
Sept. 14, 1888 - Oct. 13, 1918

C.R. Mitchell
May 23, 1871 - May 17, 1912

Molly E. Mitchell
wife of Chas. R. Mitchell
Nov. 28, 1867 - May 10, 1911

Rosie Ella Mitchell
June 12, 1901 - Mar. 30, 1935

LUMPKIN
William T.
Sept. 14, 1888 - Oct. 13, 1918

MITCHELL
William F.
Oct. 7, 1869 - Aug. 16, 1934
Phoebe S.
Feb. 27, 1867 - April 2, 1941

One Unmarked Lot

Ora Thomas Tribble Campbell
1887-1910

Robert Hawes Campbell
Mar. 24, 1879 - Dec. 31, 1960

[Infant of James Preston Campbell and
Louise Terrell; unmarked]

John Collins Tribble
1858-1907

Ella Luck Tribble
1858-1912

Albert W. Luck*

Sally A. Tribble*

---

*Moved here from the old Luck
homestead, later Onan E. Taylor's place.

This church is located near Chilesburg, Virginia, on Route 207 and 4.3 miles west of Penola, Virginia. County Line was organized in 1784, and is situated on the dividing line between Caroline and Spotsylvania counties--thus the name "County Line."

The site of the original church was .5 mile from the present one, and more towards Spotsylvania County. Membership of this church came from nearby Waller's Church of Spotsylvania County, and members of the Waller family first occupied its pulpit.

In his early days and before his conversion to the Baptist faith in 1767, John Waller belonged to the Episcopal Church. Before this he participated in persecuting the Baptists. In 1793, Waller moved to Asheville, South Carolina where he died in 1802. His brother William Edmund Waller served as the first pastor of County Line Baptist Church, but shortly thereafter removed to Kentucky.

In 1841, the old church property was sold to the Rehoboth Methodist Church, and County Line moved to a site across the road from where the cemetery is now found. In 1885, the church was relocated to its third site across the road from the cemetery. There is no evidence of graves for any early members at the site now used by the Methodists.

Visited April 24, 1963.

Frank J. Satterwhite
July 4, 1881 - December 12, 1960
Hettie L. Satterwhite
January 29, 1887 -

Silas L. Haynes
August 11, 1883 - October 22, 1962
Gertrude E. Haynes
March 16, 1891 -

Elizabeth Smith Dabney
November 2, 1902 - March 19, 1960

Kyle H. Mabes
Va. Cpl. 318 Inf. 80 Div. W.W.I.
June 14, 1887 - March 15, 1952

Joseph S. Morris
August 9, 1912 - February 16, 1955

Albert A. Furcron
1913-1952

James J. Yarbrough
Co. G, 30 Va. Inf., C.S.A.

R.F.T.
Died 1891

Unmarked Stone

Eugene T. Carneal
July 6, 1906 - April 2, 1959

Three Unmarked Stones

William N. Eldridge
1872-1951
Laura M. Eldridge
1880-1953

Maggie, wife of S.J. Walser
July 3, 1865 - February 16, 1913

Cather Moody
October 12, 1887 - October 26, 1912

33

County Line Baptist Church

Infants, son and daughter of
C.W. & J.A. Galyen

Infant son of
Carlton & Leola Taylor
May 25, 1946 - May 26, 1946

Infant daughter of
Carlton & Leola Taylor
May 25, 1946 - May 28, 1946

Six Unmarked Graves

Lila T. Morris
1873-1957

J.M. Ernest
December 4, 1851 - March 7, 1911

Emma V. Simmons
wife of J.M. Ernest
July 4, 1861 - November 28, 1924

J. Waller Ernest
September 6, 1886 - March 19, 1946

Two Graves With Cement Blocks

William H. Carter
1881-1936

Grave With Cement Block

Thomas Martin Allen
son of L.M. & A.M. Allen
Born in Gloucester, February 17, 1845
Died in Caroline, August 25, 1849

Alma E. Satterwhite
1875-1952
Maude I. Satterwhite
1883-1961

Hunter McGuire Smith
November 27, 1900-December 19, 1950
ALDA
Alta Wright Dabney
May 3, 1894 - March 1, 1940

Everett W. Dabney
July 18, 1884 - December 10, 1949

Katherine Coghill Dabney
1897-148

James T. Haynes
1886-1959
Lucy C. Haynes
1884-

Lillie L. Moody
1895-
Wade W. Moody
1887-1936

James P. Fox
1887-1949

H.L. Smith
April 2, 1848 - July 2, 1901

Fanny Payne
[illegible]

Sallie Payne
[illegible]

Lida M. Dabney
May 25, 1875 - December 4, 1950
Ruth W. Dabney
March 11, 1873 - April 15, 1951

T. Curtis Allen
November 6, 1895 - June 6, 1947

Lucy R. Allen
1868-1943
H. Marcel Allen
1860-1943

Yancy C. Galyen
March 16, 1862 - November 24, 1949
Mollie Y. Galyen
May 8, 1866 - August 4, 1941

Edith Faye Harris
November 4, 1941 - January 3, 1942

34

County Line Baptist Church

Charles E. Dickinson
October 26, 1870 - March 29, 1942

John Clair Bevans
Va. Pvt. H. Co. 1878
Engr. Avn. Bn. W.W. II
July 17, 1904 - June 24, 1962
Elizabeth B. Bevans
January 11, 1949 -

Virgie V. Pemberton
January 23, 1882 -
Lewis L. Pemberton
April 2, 1880 - January 6, 141

C. Raymond Allen
July 4, 1904 - August 12, 1926

George G. Luck
son of Joel T. & Maggie Luck
April 20, 1911
Age 10 mos. 18 days

Joel T. Luck
December 24, 1874 - November 8, 1958
Maggie S. Luck
June 21, 1879 -

S.W. Allen
November 15, 1830 - January 31, 1903

R. Emma Allen
January 19, 1834 - October 15, 1927

Capt. G. Allensworth
August 19, 1835 - July 14, 1911

Ella J. Allen
April 8, 1869 - January 25, 1920

Lewis H. Allen
husband of Ella Allen
April 12, 1870 - July 19, 1957

Frank C. Butler
Va. Pvt. 11 Inf. 5 Div.
September 3, 1943

John Wesley Carneal
May 16, 1928 - March 23, 1934

John G. Durrett
June 8, 1886 - December 18, 1936

Unmarked Grave

Grave Marked With Cement Block

Infant daughter of
J.G. & Maude Durrette
June 16, 1931

John G. Durrette
June 8, 1886 - December 18, 1936

R. Andrew Durrette
January 7, 1933 - December 29, 1948

Percy Calvert Wigglesworth
1879-1946

Eva H. Smith
July 13, 1871 - May 28, 1920

J.W. Bondurant
October 18, 1833 - March 16, 1910

Rebecca R. Bondurant
August 30, 1839 - July 7, 1901

Ida May
wife of A.G. Smith
December 14, 1858 - May 19, 1933

A.G. Smith
December 7, 1845 - August 19, 1934

Haley E. Curtis
March 20, 1891 - February 24, 1949

Thomas T. Curtis
September 19, 1869 - August 2, 1945

Mary Ann Simmons Curtis
January 14, 1845 - June 10, 1914

Joshua Curtis
December 10, 1839 - October 24, 1904

Cornelius Smith
March 2, 1899 - October 26, 1906

County Line Baptist Church

Rebecca Bondurant, infant daughter of
Ned & Bessie Campbell
April 22, 1916 - May 4, 1916

Thomas Edward Campbell
August 5, 1876 - September 13, 1937

J. Obie Peyton
October 1, 1877 - July 20, 1941

Tressie B. Peyton
January 14, 1878 - August 17, 1956

Charles H. Satterwhite
1882-1954

Unmarked Grave

Walter James Edwards
April 1, 1915 - October 1, 1932

Annie Bell S. Edwards
December 8, 1888 - October 22, 1930

Joseph W. Satterwhite
July 6, 1876 - November 13, 1925
Susan T. Satterwhite
December 16, 1884-November 16, 1950

Marcia Jane
wife of G.W. Satterwhite
July 7, 1853 - May 2, 1911

Geo. W. Satterwhite
August 2, 1850 - May 5, 1919

I.M. Satterwhite
July 18, 1875 - January 20, 1924

Beuford R. Satterwhite
son of E.L. and O.J. Satterwhite
January 9, 1920 - September 18, 1929

Frank B. Satterwhite
December 13, 1909 - October 28, 1936

Ernest L. Satterwhite
July 24, 1883 - December 25, 1942

Nana E. Runyan
March 8, 1899 - June 16, 1921

George R. Warrington
February 26, 1895 - October 12, 1943

William Warrington Hall
August 11, 1921 - June 29, 1942

Arline Fab Smith (Baby)

Arthur Lee Smith, Jr. (Baby)

Two Unmarked Graves

Lilburne Mason Smith
son of Willie & Rena Smith
February 8, 1894 - January 2, 1902

J. Willie Smith
July 14, 1861 - August 25, 1936

John Franklin Davis
March 1, 1876 - April 16, 1944

Joseph Todd Davis
February 24, 1871 - November 27, 1907

Susie V. Davis Maddox
Sept. 17, 1874 - Sept. 10, 1899

Davis G. Maddox
February 26, 1899 - July 29, 1899

A.G. Davis
June 16, 1845 - June 18, 1914
A Deacon of the Baptist Church for 40
years

Julia F. Collins
wife of A.W. Davis
June 5, 1846 - April 24, 1926

Dr. Cornelius H. Davis
son of A.W. & Julia F. Davis
July 17, 1884 - August 30, 1920
[Mason]

County Line Baptist Church

Emmett Apollas Luck
son of Emmett & Maggie Luck
February 17, 1896 - February 18, 1896

Samuel Apollos Luck
Janaury 1, 1844 - February 4, 1896

Mary Eliza Luck
April 3, 1847 - July 14, 1931

Grave With Footstone and Boxwood

Willie M. Waller
February 6, 1861 - December 28, 1942

Jennie Waller White
August 21, 1858 - January 17, 1909

Harry B. White
June 18, 1857 - September 1, 1928

Emily E. White
January 10, 1883 - January 27, 1938

E. May White
1884-1950
[Mason]

Infant daughter of
Roy B. & Marshie P. Seay
February 16, 1929

Doris Rose
daughter of Roy B. & Marshie P. Seay
August 14, 1935 - August 23, 1935

Aubrey C. Pugh
March 3, 1884 - September 26, 1926
Ida S. Pugh
January 2, 1886 -

William A. Burnett
October 21, 1935 - December 20, 1958

Earline Pugh Burnett
November 1, 1915 - July 30, 1958

Doris Rosa Pugh
November 15, 1924-September 30, 1928

Lizzie Satterwhite
December 27, 1881 - February 2, 1914

Mattie L. Satterwhite
May 16, 1890 - April 2, 1917

John B. Satterwhite
May 26, 1854 - July 31, 1917

Elvira C. Satterwhite
August 6, 1862 - February 25, 1941

Maurice C. Satterwhite
October 23, 1892 -
Grace S. Satterwhite
May 11, 1900 - February 13, 1957

Two Graves Marked by Boxwood

Mordica Thomas Sizer
1870-1930
Rosa Smith Sizer
1871-1952

Capt. Cornelius T. Smith
April 2, 1842 - December 11, 1937
Co. A 36 Bn. Va. Cav., C.S.A.

Sallie Collins
wife of Capt. C.T. Smith
November 5, 1841 - May 20, 1933
President Caroline Chapter UDC
1896-1933

Susie Smith Parker
wife of F.E. Parker
January 14, 1864 - December 27, 1912

Dr. Cornelius Timothy Smith, Jr.
August 17, 1870 - November 4, 1911

Susan W. Collins
wife of A.G. Ware
March 26, 1834 - May 31, 1910

Lee J. Smith
October 9, 1861 - January 23, 1933
Elvie Chewning Smith
April 30, 1877 - January 21, 1953

County Line Baptist Church

Mrs. Bettie Terrell Walkins
November 1, 1837 - November 15, 1922

Drusilla Davis Smith
December 19, 1875 - January 29, 1939

Lilburn Mason Smith
January 30, 1844 - March 5, 1925

William M. Waller
September 15, 1878 - June 20, 1959
Bettie H. Waller
March 4, 1891 - August 28, 1960

Olivia E. Waller
July 25, 1915 - July 12, 1916

Genevieve G. Satterwhite
November 6, 1868 - September 7, 1928
Frank D. Satterwhite
November 2, 1862 - February 12, 1934

Bessie Satterwhite
1896-1949

Myrtle Satterwhite
1892-1951

Georgianna W. Seal
wife of C.H. Durrett
July 1, 1861 - June 21, 1920

Susie Durrett
July 10, 1893 - February 11, 1915

Mary Lee Carter
September 11, 1900 - March 12, 1915
Mary Viola Carter
December 18, 1871 - January 20, 1923
Jeter G. Carter
July 8, 1870 - December 3, 1954

Infant son of
Fred W. & Annie M. Carter
June 7, 1934 - June 9, 1934

Unmarked Grave

Elton Dora Carnohan
December 22, 1874 - October 3, 1951

E. Garland Satterwhite
November 9, 1908 - September 7, 1948

Lynn A. Satterwhite
April 27, 1869 - May 24, 1947
Eddie C. Satterwhite
December 23, 1880 - April 28, 1937

E.E.H.

C.T. Humphries
March 14, 1889 - March 7, 1934

W.L. Humphries
March 2, 1883 - July 25, 1955

Hawsie D. Humphries
January 19, 1893 - April 14, 1941
Samuel J. Humphries
November 21, 1886 - February 9, 1961
Hattie W. Humphries
October 11, 1881 - February 25, 1960

Walter S. Hart
December 16, 1858 - February 15, 1925
Etta Blanton Hart
February 28, 1866 - November 14, 1941

Catharine A. Hatton
Died February 11, 1911

Clyde Alma Satterwhite
August 16, 1898 - February 12, 1957

W.W. Wright
May 9, 1842 - March 30, 1912

Mollie M. Wright
February 11, 1847 - January 20, 1915

Ruby Butler Durrett
May 7, 1896 - February 24, 1942

Less S. Butler
September 28, 1874 - February 23, 1953

William R. Butler
December 5, 1866 - February 19, 1941

County Line Baptist Church

Nellie Peyton Burruss
April 12, 1907 - June 24, 1938

Lena L. Butler
June 17, 1891 - December 15, 1928

John T. Butler
March 18, 1886 - May 11, 1956

Cora L. Satterwhite
1926-1929

Annie B. Satterwhite
1929-1930

Bessie L. Satterwhite
November 30, 1895 - May 23, 1954

John H. Satterwhite
July 8, 1887 - September 1, 1954

John F. Coffey
1877-1953

Frances H. Coffey
1874-1956

Three Graves Marked by Cement Blocks

Willie T. Spicer
1869-1952

Charlie J. Spicer
1871-1952
Lucy S. Spicer
1866-1951

George W. Spicer
July 4, 1848 - May 10, 1925
Georgiana Spicer
November 28, 1845 - December 1, 1927

Susie M. Carter
November 18, 1884 - April 17, 1944

J.E. Haynes
December 26, 1882 - March 6, 1924

Annah Gatewood
February 3, 1855 - August 14, 1926

Peggy H. Gatewood
May 13, 1868 - December 1, 1946

Charles J. Gatewood
April 28, 1866 - March 29, 1949

Clara Gatewood Smith
November 30, 1860 - March 4, 1927

James H. Smith
March 8, 1856 - April 2, 1932

Nannie Smith
March 8, 1863 - September 30, 1927

Berkeley J. Smith
1894-1950

William Henry Smith
February 9, 1890 - February 1, 1956

Lawrence Berkley Allen
July 26, 1893 - March 27, 1956

Bettie L. Allen, nee Blanton
September 20, 1855 - October 29, 1937
John T. Allen
September 17, 1854 - October 4, 1912

William Earl Allen
July 14, 1900 - June 19, 1962

Maggie D. Pemberton
1889-
William R. Pemberton
1877-1949

Mary T. Dabney
wife of F.L. Pemberton
August 21, 1886 - January 2, 1919

Frank Dabney
1859-1947
Willie Burnette Dabney
1861-1952
Benjamin Franklin Dabney
1895-1939

H. Franklin Holloway
April 10, 1915 - November 5, 1938

County Line Baptist Church

John A. Holloway
October 14, 1870 - July 5, 1935

J. Nettie Holloway
September 27, 1890 - March 17, 1930

Lola F. Holloway
January 5, 1906 - August 7, 1924

Martha Ann Holloway
March 11,1849 - April 12, 1923

Blanche, daughter of
J.L. & M.T. Seay
December 29, 1909 - May 11, 1919

Ida L. Seay
May 11, 1884 - November 26, 1935
Mary T. Seay
March 17, 1870 -

John L. Seay
January 15, 1859 - July 28, 1944

Sarah S. Seay
December 15, 1856 - January 15, 1918

George T. Seay
October 5, 1856 - September 10, 1946

Ryland A. McAllister
1892-1958

Bettie Lee McAllister
December 21, 1937 - January 6, 1938

J.R. McAllister
January 28, 1872 - April 4, 1936
Loyal Council No. 17, D. of A.

John McAllister
February 4, 1870 - June 25, 1914

Walter L. McAllister
March 9, 1868 - February 23, 1944
Bettie P. McAllister
August 27, 1871 - March 14, 1955

Baby McAllister
1922

Grave Marked With Rock

Martha J. Hall
wife of J.T. Hall
November 9, 1875 - July 11, 1918

James T. Hall
May 10, 1875 - December 21, 1950

Willie James Haynes
October 26, 1874 - October 24, 1940

Ivan Stuart
son of Willie & Frances Haynes
October 17, 1914 - August 21, 1922

Willie Mason Haynes
February 6, 1916 - May 21, 1944

Hazel Lee Williams
July 2, 1947 - August 4, 1947

Lloyd Linwood Carter
March 21, 1913 - February 27, 1960
Aileen Lowry Carter
July 28, 1914 -
Married March 21, 1945

Eliza B. Carter
April 29, 1877 - December 25, 1945

John J. Carter
January 10, 1879 - April 9, 1948

Ida McLean Minton
June 11, 1880 - November 10, 1944

Robert R. Wright
Va. Pvt. 1 Cl., 318 Inf. 80 Div.
June 18, 1895 - January 18, 1944
Nettie F. Wright
October 23, 1893 -

Lotus F. Wright
May 27, 1925 - October 29, 1947

Lillie C. Payne
March 28, 1881 - June 19, 1948

40

County Line Baptist Church

W. Russell Seay
July 2, 1882 - September 8, 1949

Carl Wayne Seay
1952-1952

Angelina Seay
1880-1955

Emmett Seay
1882-1954

Mary E. Anderson
December 11, 1891 -
Frederick G. Anderson
October 16, 1880 - June 17, 1946

Jackie Mae
daughter of Ernest & Virginia Haynes
November 7, 1942 - September 14, 1949

S. George Warrington
March 15, 1869 - January 29, 1946

Malvina W. Warrington
September 29, 1873 - February 9, 1949

William Jackson Luck
July 4, 1861 - November 6, 1931

Lucy J. Butler Luck
December 14, 1867-September 25, 1948

Elsie M. Burruss
May 27, 1916 -
Louis L. Burruss
April 10, 1906 - April 26, 1954

Arthur G. Pemberton
November 3, 1880 - July 29, 1946
Lillie F. Pemberton
November 22, 1887 -

Walter C. Butler
September 17, 1869 - April 19, 1954
Nannie E. Butler
February 14, 1873 - June 28, 1949

David Nathan Cardwell
April 16, 1878 - May 11, 1955

Ida Hamby Cardwell
August 16, 1892 -

Clyde Joseph Cecil
July 17, 1929 - August 21, 1959

George Grayson Seay
July 26, 1940 - August 21, 1959

Kate K. Feeney
April 19, 1865 - November 14, 1960

Lorina Hamby Walsh
1882-1962

Unmarked Grave

Mrs. Grace Jones Stanley
April 22, 1963
Age 65

Anthony Alan Lane
1961-1962

Charles Wayne Lane
1953-1954

Allie W. Hart
November 28, 1890 - June 27, 1958

John W. Allen
August 22, 1877 - June 9, 1952
Mary W. Allen
August 8, 1875 - March 6, 1949

Thelma S. Allen
September 12, 1912-November 13, 1948

James Maudie Pugh
March 13, 1886 - August 2, 1950

Milton C. Pugh
January 8, 1950 - October 11, 1958

Baby Boy Pugh
1958-1958

Charles G. Hart
July 6, 1889 - March 7, 1959

41

Site of Emmaus Christian Church

Located .1 mile north of Old Penola post office on Route 601. Emmaus Christian Church was established in 1837 as a branch of Antioch Christian Church. The first members were former members of Antioch, three men and four women, who met during the winter months in a school house across from Palestine Farm on the south side of Polecat Creek. In the summer, members collected under an arbor of an ancient oak across the road. This oak still stands at the left of the entry gate of Palestine Farm. Church services were always subject to cancellation due to inclement weather.

As a permanent site the congregation in 1838 erected a meeting house on the north side of Polecat Creek. The building was singular in construction, the floor being sloped on a inclined plane, two thirds of which rose from 2 to 3 feet in height and 20 feet in length to accommodate the speaker in the pulpit.

Emmaus Christian Church burned to the ground during an ice storm on the first Sunday in February 1943 and was never rebuilt. The fire started where the flue ran through the roof and could not be extinguished because of downed telephone lines. The site is now marked by two sets of cement steps. To the rear and left of the building site is the cemetery which is overgrown in honeysuckle. Many graves here are unmarked.

The only records known to exist for this church are deposed at the Virginia Historical Society, with a copy in the Virginia State Library. These records begin after the Civil War; the earlier records having been destroyed by soldiers of the Union Army.

This site was visited in 1953.

Thomas Barclay Jeter*
1871-1941

Blanche Beazley Jeter*
1879-1937

Joseph Ashbury Sanford**
January 26, 1877 - December 28, 1945

Lillian H. Sanford
August 7, 1903 - December 18, 1926

Lucy Dew Davis
August 7, 1903 - September 3, 1925

Fanny Dew
February 19, 1844 - February 22, 1926

Dr. Philip A. Dew
September 20, 1840-September 19, 1893

Mary W. Dew
1869-1936

Philip A. Dew
January 21, 1865 - August 12, 1929

Our Baby
Mary Eliz. Dew
Died April 9, 1908

Eugene B. Jeter
October 28, 1901 - November 20, 1925

Eulalia Hargrave Johnson
October 28, 1863 - July 26, 1921

Site of Emmaus Christian Church

O.W. Sutton
February 22, 1827 - November 5, 1872

Gertrude Dew Reynolds
Died July 3, 1901

Lydia A. Carson
July 24, 1829 - July 4, 1891

Maggie B. Carson
August 8, 1885 - May 20, 1905

Cyrus Carson
February 20, 1824 - April 6, 1902

———————————

*Moved to Greenlawn Cemetery, Bowling Green, Virginia, in 1963.
**Moved to Corinth Christian Church Cemetery, King William County, Virignia, in 1963.

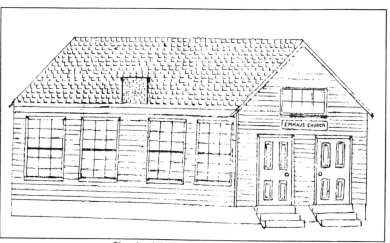

Sketch of Emmaus Christian Church

43

In the first half of the 18th century a considerable number of Quakers purchased land in Caroline County, and began meetings at Golansville, sometimes called the Caroline Meeting. Established on land acquired by John Cheadle from Thomas Carr in 1733, the meeting house was built in 1739 as part of the Cedar Creek Monthly Meeting. After having lasted 114 years, the meeting discontinued holding services at this site in 1853.

John Cheadle was the first secretary of the meeting house; succeeded by Samuel Hargrave when Cheadle died in 1874. Some members of this meeting house moved to North Carolina in 1853. Many of those who remained in Caroline later united with Emmaus Christian Church at Penola, Virginia.

In back of what was once the white clapboard house that was used for worship, was found a Quaker burying ground. It was in a fenced area, now covered with ivy and periwinkle, and beneath maple and paulownia trees. As was the custom with Quakers, there are no grave markers. Another Quaker burying ground existed on the Ness family place in the triangle formed by the roads leading between Chilesburg, Blanton and Partlow. Still others exist at Quaker homesites, such as the Chiles family cemetery, now part of "Chandlers," just off Route 601 and near Penola, Virginia.

The records of this meeting house are now in the manuscript collection of the Valentine Museum in Richmond, Virginia. Marshall Wingfield, in his History of Caroline County, Virginia, page 478, provided that: *Dr. Terrell, his mother and father and other members of the family are buried at Golansville, Caroline county, in the little burying ground which adjoined the Quaker Meeting House that formerly stood there.*

TERRELL, Elizabeth Harris, wife of Samuel Terrell.
TERRELL, George Fox, physician, son of Samuel Terrell and Elizabeth Harris, died at the age of 37 years.
TERRELL, Samuel, was married to Elizabeth Harris on May 7, 1800. We find in William Wade Henshaw's Encyclopedia of American Quaker Genealogy, Volume VI, Henrico Monthly Meeting (page 215) and Cedar Creek Monthly Meeting (page 276), that Samuel Terrell, of Caroline County, son of Pleasant Terrell, was granted permission on April 12th to marry at the Richmond Meeting House to Elizabeth Harris, daughter of James of Richmond, Virginia.

Grace Episcopal Church

Located 11.5 miles north of Bowling Green, Virginia, at the intersection of routes 2 and 612, at Corbin, Virginia. Grace Episcopal Church was established in 1832. The present structure is the original building. The first rector of this church was William Friend who is commemorated with a small monument inside the church and which reads: In Memoriam-- William Friend, Rector of this Church for 38 years. Rev. Friend is buried in the churchyard of St. Peter's Episcopal Church in Port Royal, Virginia.

During the Civil War this church was used as a hospital for wounded soldiers, many of whom were buried here. After the war, the graves of these soldiers were removed elsewhere. As a result of dwindling attendance, the church disbanded many years ago and is now used by another demonimation, although still owned by the Episcopal Church.

This site was visited December 2, 1961.

Tazwell Tayloe Corbin
Sept. 27, 1907 - Aug. 26, 1958

John Gatchell Corbin
Mar. 1, 1897 - Mar. 10, 1953

Sarah Gatchell Corbin
Aug. 26, 1871 - Nov. 26, 1955

Champe Carter Corbin
Feb. 25, 1864 - Mar. 31, 1950

Champe Carter Corbin
wife of Carter Stevenson Gordon
July 16, 1903 - Jan. 23, 1941

William A. Hennig
1830-1919

Sacred to the Memory of Jane
beloved wife of the Rev. Henry Wall,
Rector of this Church
She died Feb. 19, 1854 in the 35th
year of her age,
leaving her bereaved husband and
two helpless children to mourn
her untimely loss.

Theodore Olin Linthicum
beloved husband of Amelia Linthicum
Nov. 11, 1901
Age 42 years

Amelia Linthicum
wife of Theodore Olin Linthicum
Oct. 18, 1946
Age 84 years

Hattie Mason
dau. of James C. and Annie M. Dickenson
Aug. 24, 1868 - Feb. 26, 1939

Thomas Buckner
son of James C. and Annie M. Dickenson
Oct. 1, 1869 - July 6, 1937

Lelia F. Yerby
1866-1947

Helen Yerby
1867-1948

45

Located .7 mile on Route 608 from Route 301 at Fort A.P. Hill. Greenlawn cemetery was established by the U.S. Government in 1941 to accommodate the graves moved from Upper Zion Baptist Church, Bethesda Baptist Church, Liberty Baptist Church, and Zoar Baptist Church, as well as the private family cemeteries on the properties which the Government acquired for the military camp. Removal of the bodies was done under direction of L.R. "Jack" Davis, a local undertaker in Bowling Green, Virginia.

Upper Zion Baptist Church was located 125 yards northeast of Upper Zion Post Office, and 9 miles northeast of Bowling Green, on Route 622. The church was torn down by the Government in 1941.

Bethesda Baptist Church was located 3.4 miles northwest of Rappahannock Academy on the south side of Route 614. This church was also torn down by the Government in 1941.

Liberty Baptist Church was located 6.2 miles southwest of Rappahannock Academy on the west side of Route 614, 1 mile east of Mica, Virginia. Now located within the boundaries of the A.P. Hill Military Reservation, the building still stands and is used as an Army chapel.

Zoar Baptist Church, organized in 1835, has been torn down.

The records of each of the four churches were sent to the Baptist Historical Society, University of Richmond, for safe keeping. Each church selected a section in the new cemetery on the land donated by the Government. The money received from the sale of the churches to the Government was used to establish a trust fund for the cemetery. Bethesda placed an endowment of $3,000 for upkeep of their portion. Through the efforts of Frank E. Bowie and L.R. Davis, these churches also erected a chapel in the center of the cemetery. The charts which L.R. Davis used in removing the graves are now at the Caroline County Historical Society, and the card file for the same is at Mann's Funeral Home, Bowling Green, Virginia.

John Montgomery Garrett
March 27, 1893-September 10, 1956

Ora Wright Gravatt

John Cherbury Gravatt
1798-1875

Amanda Broaddus Gravatt
1807-1889

George W. Marshall
2 Lieut. 47 Va. Inf., C.S.A.
May 5, 1872, aged 44 years

Polly Marshall
Died February 2, 1890
aged 57 years

Sarah E. Marshall
Wife of John W. Marshall
March 18, 1837 - March 27, 1887

Greenlawn Cemetery

John Glassell Marshall
November 30, 1882-November 29, 1955

J.H. Marshall
Co. H, 30 Va. Inf., C.S.A.

Ten Unmarked Marshall Graves

William George White
February 2, 1872 - March 9, 1932

Margaret Ada Kay
August 3, 1886 - April 13, 1941

Annie Rodgers Kay
July 10, 1883 - May 17, 1945

Willard P. Kay
May 28, 1905, in the 52nd year of age

Ada Gravatt, wife of Willard Kay
October 25, 1850 - January 25, 1928

Arthur Merle Kay
October 17, 1877 - July 17, 1938

Willard K. Andrews, Jr.
1945-1961

Elmer L. Cook
1891-1947

Frank G. Cook
November 24, 1897-September 11, 1938

Ruby S. Mitchell wife of Frank G. Cook
August 29, 1900 - November 15, 1935

Alice S. Cook
1873-1955

Davis L. Cook
1869-1949

Phebe A. Smoot
November 30, 1837 - May 26, 1906
Annie B. Wright
October 2, 1860-December 9, 1881
F.G. Cook - Grandson
Sarah D. Smoot
March 9, 1866 - August 11, 1878
Benjamin F. Smoot, Sr.
June 27, 1835 - February 20, 1907

Calvin N. Houston
August 18, 1841 - September 20, 1922

Diliah C. Houston,
wife of C.N. Houston
July 1, 1851 - June 28, 1919

Kate Lee Houston,
daughter of F.M. & C.B. Houston
January 23, 1911 - October 25, 1913

Hannah B. McCarthy
1873-1957

Robert L. McCarthy
1862-1941

Edwin M. Andrews, Sr.
May 4, 1881-December 17, 1946

Linda K. Andrews
December 9, 1880 - July 4, 1948

Edwin Andrews
Corp. 30 Va. Inf., C.S.A.
1834 - September 1897

Sallie M. Ferneyhough, his wife
1849-1914

Grover C. Houston
1884-1936

Mrs. Ruffin

Almo Carter

Henry J. Motley
December 6, 1872 - January 17, 1939

47

Greenlawn Cemetery

Clara B. Motley
August 2, 1871 - June 8, 1936

Helen W. Motley
February 15, 1883-September 23, 1960

Alfred Fuller Wright
1854-1936

Hannah Motley Wright
1860-1935

Unmarked Grave

Infant Wright
1917

Infant Wright
1923

Willie Wright
1865-1933

Mrs. Jim Wright

Bradford G. Carter
1884-1947

Lizzie H. Carter
1884-1959

John B. Hicks
August 22, 1851 - June 18, 1925

Etta L. Hicks
July 29, 1855 - May 17, 1926

Joseph Hart Hicks
September 17, 1882-December 18, 1951

Annie Houston Hicks
March 16, 1888 - March 9, 1960

John P. Ruppert
January 25, 1942 - August 19, 1960

Robert Lee Jones
March 13, 1881 - July 13, 1946

Henry Jones

Ella Jones

Beauman Jones

M.H. Jones
May 13, 1866 - March 6, 1952

Luther Harold Kay
October 17, 1926 - August 28, 1943

Luther T. Kay
February 24, 1876 - June 15, 1956

Mattie W. Kay
August 19, 1900 -

Infant Motley

Infant Motley

Bertie Lynwood Parr
1875-1945

Lulie Kay Parr
1883-1953

William H. Brooks
September 6, 1871 - January 23, 1938

Ned Parr

Unmarked Grave

William B. Bruce
1853-1930

Fannie B. Bruce
1858-1931

Buenavista Bruce
June 20, 1847 - March 19, 1928

Rosa B. Bruce
1857 - October 19, 1892

Warren B. Bruce
November 19, 1880-December 24, 1961

Greenlawn Cemetery

Infant Bruce

Infant

Infant

Infant

Lucy C. Bruce
wife of M.J. Bruce, Jr.
June 10, 1865 - March 10, 1930
M.J. Bruce
April 7, 1859 - November 27, 1939

Percy Cecil Bruce
November 8, 1888 - June 9, 1957

Gay Brooks Bruce
April 7, 1897 -

John E. Samuel
November 13, 1886 -
Mollie K. Samuel
November 18, 1879 - June 11, 1962

William Stuart McKay, Sr.
January 25, 1903 - May 11, 1954
[Mason]

William Stuart McKay, Jr.
son of Wm. S. & Alma McKay
1927-1932

Leon H. Bruce
February 12, 1906 - August 16, 1927

Joseph H. Bruce
December 24, 1880 - February 27, 1945
Annie L. Bruce
May 20, 1878 - April 26, 1953

William Henry Houston
1890-1918

Alice Ruth Carter

Mark Beal Tignor
April 21, 1892 - September 22, 1956
Mary Alice Tignor
April 14, 1898 - April 23, 1958

Clarence B. Wright
February 22, 1883 - August 8, 1948
Jeannette L. Wright
April 1, 1891 - February 17, 1953

Jennie Allport

Willie Allport

Martha Houston

G.L. Houston

Della P. Houston
January 1, 1873 - December 15, 1922

Maria Gray

William E. Gray
Co. B, 9 Va. Cav., C.S.A.

Virginia H. Fuqua
October 13, 1896 - April 20, 1922

Henry Whittaker
Pvt. 30 Va. Inf., C.S.A.
April 14, 1912

John W. Pitts
August 22, 1902 - December 4, 1941

George H. Pitts
May 14, 1854 - November 30, 1937

Lucy B. Pitts
June 2, 1871 - June 2, 1951

George G. Pitts
son of Geo. H. & Virginia Pitts
January 10, 1883 - December 10, 1916

Henry M. Pitts
son of Geo. H. & Virginia Pitts
September 7, 1891 - October 17, 1918
He gave His Life for his Country.

Julius C. Sale
1851-1927

49

Greenlawn Cemetery

Sue E. Sale
1861-1941

Seddon Jackson Bruce
August 22, 1887 - June 10, 1952
Emma Trice Bruce
May 13, 1891 -

Winston S. Bruce
July 9, 1910 - August 29, 1910

Essie Gravatt Motley
May 27, 1886 - October 3, 1962
Willie Bowie Motley
March 10, 1884 -

Bettie F. Gravatt
February 14, 1850 - February 7, 1912

Andrew J. Gravatt
Sgt. Co. C, 47 Va. Inf., C.S.A.

William Ancel Gravatt
March 4, 1884 - November 23, 1957

Infant Pitts

Infant Pitts

Virginia L. Pitts
wife of Geo. H. Pitts
November 14, 1862 - January 28, 1898

John N. Motley
November 9, 1853 - March 20, 1926

James T. Gravatt
1862-1924
Sarah G. Gravatt
1865-1954

Annie B. Gravatt
1888-1916

Willie Garrett

Fleetwood Garrett

Edmonia Gouldman

PARKER

Charles A. Gouldman
August 15, 1883 - March 9, 1956

Lulie Gravatt Gouldman
August 14, 1856 - October 31, 1921
Charles M. Gouldman
December 26, 1853 - November 1, 1930

Edith Gouldman Powers
December 13, 1885 - April 26, 1936

Eugenia G. Anderson
1887-1945

Hampton W. Anderson
1884-1950

Richard Gouldman

Infant Gouldman

Asa Gouldman

Haseltine Gouldman

John Gouldman

Emelie Gouldman

Jasper Carter

Lucy Oliver Carter

Ann Gouldman

Richard Gouldman

Bettie Samuel

WHITTAKER

Infant Whittaker

Infant Whittaker

Maria Whittaker

Cordelia Carter

50

Greenlawn Cemetery

Infant Carter

Unmarked Grave

A. Marline Gray
January 24, 1937 - February 28, 1937

Melville D. Gray
1899-1944

Alice H. Gray
1898-1945

Charlie B. Brooks
1869-1902
Bettie A. Brooks
1866-1948
Mary E. Brooks, his mother
1815-1901

Richard Hunter
1889-1916

Laura Baynham
1886-1917

Rogers S. Wright
October 24, 1921 - November 5, 1921

Stanley Oben
1898-1928

Judith B. Oben
1896-1946

Nancy R. Wright
May 6, 1854 - July 2, 1922

John B. Wright
March 13, 1837 - April 15, 1922

Annie L. Henderson
July 18, 1875 - April 28, 1934

John R. Wright
December 4, 1884 - May 19, 1953

Frankie Gray Wright
wife of John R. Wright
February 19, 1894 - April 18, 1951

John W. Wright
August 5, 1920 - May 24, 1944

Eddie B. Wright
January 9, 1877 - August 20, 1948
Rockie B. Wright
October 22, 1885 -

Idelle Wright
wife of John R. Wright
July 26, 1880 - February 12, 1907

Ervin Pollard
April 18, 1903 - June 19, 1942
[Mason]

Mollie F. Beazley
wife of L.B. Brooks
1862-1933

Luther Baynham
1853-1924

Winston Stuart Wright
February 14, 1913 - June 2, 1934

Edith E. Gray
1871-1961
Charles L. Gray
1860-1935

Mollie C. Gray
wife of Geo. W. Gray
May 17, 1860 - July 18, 1920

George W. Gray
May 2, 1858 - March 25, 1930
(by his son M.D. Gray)

Hazel M. Gray
December 9, 1930 - April 25, 1937

Cornelius B. Gray
1890-1959
Nannie Gay W. Gray
1896-

Russell Gray
June 4, 1914 - September 29, 1934

Greenlawn Cemetery

Edwin Gray
December 3, 1929 - January 11, 1935

Calvin E. Loving
December 1872 - January 1919
Susie F. Loving
October 1870 - February 1948

Lewis H. Carter
1881-1943

Ellwood M. Gray
February 1, 1899 -
Gladys Bruce Gray
January 10, 1900 - June 21, 1960

Harry Luther
April 28, 1882 - August 4, 1934

Almyra Virginia Beazley
1868-1915

O'Jennings Beazley
1866-1947

Hannah H. Beazley
1879-1957

Lyell Hunter Wright
December 12, 1916-September 22, 1956

James H. Wright
April 30, 1885 - July 26, 1943
Lillian B. Wright
May 8, 1885 -

Lonie May Carter

Bernard Carter

Sallie Carter

Infant Carter

Mor. W. Cole
Corp. 30 Va. Inf., C.S.A.
January 10, 1904

Perry Tolcott Wright
June 12, 1869 - December 15, 1928

Fannie B. Motley

Charles H. Motley
1852-1934

Luther A. Carter
June 11, 1844 - April 29, 1903

Lucy A. Carter, nee Haynes
June 11, 1847 - March 24, 1918

Andrew Jackson Carter
May 12, 1880 - December 23, 1960

Thomas A. Samuel
October 29, 1856 - October 16, 1931

Robert Seldon Garnett
October 27, 1848 - April 24, 1938

William G. Garnett
1823-1899
Jane S. Garnett
1830-1915

Emma S. Garnett
1862-1926

Joseph E. Penny
1886-1956
Beatrice C. Penny
1896-

Dewey R. Wright
October 25, 1898 - May 20, 1942

Cornelia A. Wright
wife of Wiley M. Wright
October 10, 1852 - March 28, 1922
Wiley M. Wright
October 30, 1844 - March 3, 1924
Pvt. 47 Va. Inf., C.S.A.

Willie B. Samuel
1885-1951

Ella F. Brooks
March 25, 1859 - November 17, 1926

Greenlawn Cemetery

Benjamin F. Brooks
January 17, 1863 - June 24, 1940

Ella Adams Brooks
March 25, 1859 - November 17, 1926

Chandos S. Penny
November 19, 1883 - March 17, 1962
Ethel V. Penny
June 25, 1894 -

Norman R. Penny
August 24, 1921 - February 6, 1936

Lucy A. Andrews
1833-1916

W.G. Andrews
January 18, 1844 - February 7, 1909

Elmyra Watts
1892-1931
Willie P. Watts
1890-1958

William L. Andrews
1863-1931

Ross Carter
1859-1883

Mariah Carter
1906-1867

Roland Carter
1871-1958

Hallie B. Carter
January 14, 1856 - February 11, 1943

Philip H. Carter
Pvt. 2 Bn. Va. Res., C.S.A.
December 23, 1811 - August 7, 1887

Emaline S. Carter
December 30, 1833 - August 15, 1890

Infant of Mr. & Mrs. Campbell
March 15, 1952

E. Leola Campbell
June 30, 1890 - January 9, 1939

Miss Hassie A. Carter
December 18, 1861 - July 7, 1917

T. Judson Carter
January 19, 1958 - February 4, 1942

Ruth Wright Carter
1886 - 1942

Erle C. Broaddus
July 11, 1893 - August 8, 1959

Robert Wright
Pvt. 47 Inf., C.S.A.
December 13, 1918

Robert Preston Wright
1890-1955

Pattie Virginia Eagar
1851-1906

Rowland Henry Eagar
1858-1927

Nettie Wright Eagar
1876-1950

Maurice Grady Clarke
1891-1947

Jennie Clarke Seymour
1885-1946

Virginia A. Clarke
1924-1877

John Eagar
1816-1899

Erasmus S. Broaddus
April 13, 1879 - September 13, 1929
Bernice W. Broaddus
October 18, 1882 -

George W. Broaddus
Corp. Co. F 30 Va. Inf., C.S.A.

Greenlawn Cemetery

Ophie E. Broaddus
wife of T.S. Jones
January 9, 1861 - February 12, 1902

Tomasia J. Mills
March 10, 1845 - October 22, 1942

James J. Broaddus
January 15, 1865 - September 24, 1950

Elizabeth Broaddus
wife of James H. Kay
March 1874 - January 1949

Ellen Odessa Broaddus
April 13, 1869 - January 24, 1899

George C. Broaddus
January 12, 1876 - August 21, 1900

Lissie R.
wife of G.W. Broaddus
1838-1915

Andrew L. Mills
Co. E 25 Va. Inf., C.S.A.

Pallison B. Mills
1st Sgt. Co. G 23 Va. Inf., C.S.A.

Clara Wright Collier
Died December 21, 1961, age 35

Everett Lee Ayers
Died December 1948

Unmarked Grave

Infant Ayers

Infant Ayers

Infant Ayers

Nora Ayers

John Ayers

Infant Chandler

Tim Chandler

J. Woody Wright
1852-1933

Mary Emma Wright
1850-1936

Thomas E. Johnson
Va Cpl 62 CM Gen Service Co WW II
July 2, 1927 - August 31, 1948

Everett C. Carter
Va. Pvt. Co. K 186 Inf. WW I
January 17, 1889 - April 16, 1960

Pearl Procter Carter
July 28, 1899 -

William B. Whittaker
Va. Pvt. 132 Field Arty. Bn.
October 24, 1914 - July 22, 1946

Three Unmarked Graves

Andrew Jackson Carter
July 9, 1953

Grace M. Carter
1883-1958

G.A. Gray

Owen Beazley

William Sutherlin

Kate Proctor

Mattie Proctor

Four Graves Marked G.A. Gray

Two Unmarked Graves

Infant Whittaker

WHITTAKER

Maude Whittaker

Greenlawn Cemetery

Eustace M. Penny
December 28, 1872-November 29, 1947

Nancy Pearl Fisher
January 11, 1954 - Age 31

George R. Carter
October 14, 1891 - July 12, 1950

Harvey "Jack" Scott Carter
February 17, 1902 - August 24, 1962

Henry G. Wright
1881-1939

Bettie I. Carter
August 7, 1869 - September 4, 1946

John G. Carter
January 19, 1865 - January 26, 1933

George W. Wright
Pvt. 30 Va. Inf., C.S.A.
January 29, 1907

Mary Jane Wright
1836-1911

Edgar B. Carter
December 2, 1896 - December 5, 1929

Herbert Gay Carter
Va. Pvt. Q.M. Corps. W.W. I
February 2, 1893 - March 29, 1948

Ida Motley Shaddock
1877-1952

Frederick Clyde Shaddock
1872-1952

Annie Dew Shaddock
1903-1957

Betsey Shaddock

Eugene Shaddock

James Shaddock

Dorothy Boulware

Lucy Long Wright

Harry Wright

Caroline Broaddus Boulware
1834-1913

James Boulware
1 Lieut. Co. B, 9 Va. Cav., C.S.A.

Eugene Boulware
1866-1872

Frances Boulware
1780-1870

Mark Boulware
Died 1811

Molly Boulware

Richard Boulware
Died 1827

James L. Boulware
1875-1947
Nellie B. Boulware
1887 -

W.L. Andrews
Copr. Co. H, 30 Va. Inf., C.S.A.

Milly Boulware
Died 1790

Richard Boulware
1783-1851

Sgt. Turner Boulware
1792-1872

Elliott Boulware
1788-1861

Agatha Saunders Boulware
Died 1836

55

Greenlawn Cemetery

James Boulware
1799-1927

Battaile Boulware
Died 1902

Lynch Wright

Allie Shaddock

Dora Shaddock

Kate L. Martin
January 6, 1883 - October 6, 1949
Harry Martin
February 28, 1877 - February 7, 1959

Robert Carter

Margaret Martin

Infant Martin

Rena Gravatt Andrews
1873-1935

Richard B. Andrews
1870-1935

L. Wesley Southworth
August 26, 1898 - December 2, 1958

Mrs. Cecil Andrews

George Allen Gray
May 22, 1886 - January 8, 1953
Hausie Carter Gray
October 15, 1888 -

Christine Broaddus

William W. Broaddus

W.S. Campbell

Crissie R. Broaddus
July 9, 1864 - May 20, 1944

Lucy C. Campbell

Cornelius C. Broaddus
1867-1948

Alice Bruce Huffines
January 15, 1889 - January 23, 1955

Claude Grover Huffines
November 27, 1884 - September 7, 1959

Ryan Garnett Wright
1896-1957
Leslie Carneal Wright
1898-

Fred Motley Shaddock
September 28, 1905 -
Jessie Acors Shaddock
July 14, 1913 - May 1, 1960

Lee Gordon Smithers
July 22, 1960 - August 23, 1960

Benjamin B. Smithers
January 27, 1887 -
Bertha H. Smithers
October 19, 1889 - June 13, 1958

John W. Newton
May 7, 1887 -
Maude M. Newton
February 5, 1893 -
Cora Lee Newton
May 7, 1885 - July 17, 1962

Elezar L. Farmer
March 10, 1882 -
Annie G. Farmer
October 1, 1892 - July 21, 1962

Marian Barlow Taylor
December 26, 1962

John W. Beazley, Jr.
1866-1937
[Mason]
Lelia C. Beazley
1877-1917

John W. Beazley III

56

Greenlawn Cemetery

Linda A. Morgan
September 13, 1948-September 15,
1948

Harold
son of Claude & Alice Huffines

George W. Moore
August 1, 1873 - April 21, 1948
Hauzie W. Moore
April 24, 1883 - May 6, 1955

W. Aubrey Wright
1886-1962
Virgie W. Wright
1889-

Harry Murdock Beazley
February 15, 1883 - April 12, 1955
Leola Hall Beazley
December 18, 1906 -

Lou Beasley

J.R. Beasley

Joseph A. Beazley
June 8, 1876 - December 3, 1940

Lawrence P. Beasley
April 22, 1882 - January 24, 1955
Sallie V. Beasley
February 24, 1896 - June 5, 1958

Unmarked Grave

James Edward Whittaker

Lernie Whittaker

Virginia Whittaker

George Whittaker

Five Beazley Graves

Mattie Lou Beazley
Born and Died 1935

Infant Beazley

John Beasley, Jr.

John Beasley, Sr.

BEASLEY

Orris Beasley

Joseph Ayers
August 10, 1896 - August 23, 1950

Earl Ayers

Hilda Ayers

Louise Howard

Dorothy Howard

Bly Howard

S. Alice Howard

L.F. Bruce

Mary H. Bruce

William Bruce

Infant Bruce

Infant Bruce

Infant Bruce

Mary Bruce

18 Graves Marked "R.L. Jones"

Unmarked Grave

Unmarked Grave

2 Graves Marked "B.A. Whittaker"

13 Graves Marked "S.B. Farmer"

Linwood Whittaker

Greenlawn Cemetery

Callie M. Farmer
February 8, 1892 - October 5, 1961
Fannie E. Farmer
August 4, 1898 -

E.F. Farmer
Age 85

Samuel L. Farmer
May 3, 1835 - July 3, 1913

Robert C. Bruce
October 6, 1889 - August 4, 1908

Ida Bruce
Age 23

Two Stones Without Markings

Steven Lewis Farmer
March 22, 1919 - June 1, 1930

Moses H. Morris
June 18, 1849 - December 24, 1917
Pearl Morris
April 13, 1873 - March 31, 1952

Child's Grave Without Marking

Unmarked Grave

J. Leonard Garner
March 6, 1898 - November 11, 1945

"Reubin Howard and Family"

William Grimes
1864-1926

Judson Howard

Joseph E. Penny

Joseph R. Penny

Florence A. Penny

John C. Minor

Margaret Selph

Sallie Selph

Jarrin Selph, Jr.

Juin Selph

John Selph

Charles F. Jordan
February 21, 1859 - January 31, 1935
Lucy O. Jordan
1858 - January 25, 1935

Charles Murray Jordan
December 18, 1880 - March 4, 1960

Elizabeth Stern

Francis C. Stern

Phebe Selph

SELPH

Richard C. Carter
1882-1951

Blanche P. Carter
1870-1951

George W. Pickett
December 25, 1886 - April 18, 1952

Maria Howard

Jim Howard

Bettie Howard

Mannie Chandler

Lola Pickett

Infant Pickett

Larry Cobel Pickett
1953 - age 42

Unmarked Grave

Greenlawn Cemetery

Minnie Wharton
January 9, 1940

Mary Wharton Loving
wife of James Woody Loving
1878-1960

C.E. Toombs
1890-1953

R.L. Toombs
1903-1955

Wallace Scott Whittaker
June 1, 1892 - June 2, 1939

Everett L. Whittaker
August 28, 1914 - May 9, 1931

Charlie Whittaker

Mrs. D.P. Toombs
January 1910 - January 1960

Jurdan Toombs

Mrs. Virginia Toombs

Franklin V. Toombs
August 18, 1920 - July 9, 1952

Maggie Kirk

Nettie Chandler

Infant Toombs

Paul C. Acors

Robert H. Puller
September 26, 1892 - February 13, 1945

Oliver D. Upshaw
April 5, 1898 -
Evelyn V. Upshaw
May 1, 1912 - August 7, 1955

Dorris Scott Vaughan
May 28, 1914 - July 29, 1958

John A. Vaughan
1874-1945
Sadie Virginia Vaughan
December 29, 1962

Lucille Vaughan
wife of William O. Hutt
February 19, 1897 - September 15, 1923

William H. Vaughan
February 27, 1869 - November 4, 1949
Theresa Marshall Vaughan
July 18, 1871 - January 2, 1947

Bessie T. Vaughan
February 24, 1916 - March 19, 1926

George Bullock

Mattie Green

Mary Louise Bullock

Mary Eliza Bullock

Catherine Jeter

Miss L.K.B. Holloway
July 30, 1831 - April 3, 1909

Elizabeth Martin

John W. Holloway
Co. K, 2 Ga. Cav., C.S.A.

Betty Susan Raines
wife of John W. Holloway
February 14, 1844 - January 6, 1917

G.W. Trice
April 8, 1806 - February 1, 1868
Pastor of Liberty Church for 20 years

James I. Bradley
February 5, 1859 - August 4, 1915

Martha T. Bradley
January 18, 1817 - December 8, 1889

59

Greenlawn Cemetery

Thornton H. Bradley
August 7, 1812 - November 9, 1904

Elliott M. Richerson
1823 - November 21, 1891

Mary Kay
wife of Elliott M. Richerson
October 9, 1822 - May 7, 1889

Lucy Richerson
wife of William H. Vaughan, Sr.
January 1, 1846 - June 9, 1906

William H. Vaughan, Sr.
August 22, 1831 - November 21, 1899

Carrie Sanford Vaughan
1880-1913
Joseph C. Vaughan, Jr.
1911-1916

Infant of E.E. Vaughan

Infant of E.E. Vaughan

Infant of J.C. Vaughan

Infant of J.C. Vaughan

Infant Vaughan

Infant of E.T. Vaughan

Infant of E.T. Vaughan

Joseph C. Vaughan
July 15, 1878 -

Donna Morris Vaughan
October 17, 1876 - February 24, 1950

Elliott T. Vaughan, Jr.
February 15, 1906 - April 20, 1944

Minnie Jackson Gravatt
wife of E.T. Vaughan
1869-1934

Elliott T. Vaughan
March 8, 1865 - May 15, 1947

Infant of William B. and Lucy B. Vaughan
November 21, 1952-November 24, 1952

George Welford Taylor
August 11, 1893 - September 2, 1952

Mary Kathryn Haynes
wife of Ellis Wellford Taylor
December 15, 1961 - January 28, 1932

Ellis Welford Taylor
December 28, 1860 - August 20, 1945

Onan E. Taylor
March 8, 1896 - April 30, 1954
Annie V. Taylor
January 20, 1899 -

B.C. Shackelford

Unmarked Grave

Lynwood C. Wright
1891-1915

Clyde L. Wright
1886-1911

R. Walter Wright
October 12, 1860 - March 19, 1901
Sallie C. Wright
November 19, 1857 - June 15, 1938

Charlie B. Wright
1895-1896

Isaac Raines

Catherine Raines

John W. Raines

John J. Raines
1849-1914
Ella G. Raines
1851-1938

60

Greenlawn Cemetery

Annella R. Raines
May 12, 1897 - August 12, 1918

R.I. "Mike" Raines
May 9, 1884 - March 1, 1949

Three Graves Marked Liberty Church

William C. Pitman
December 18, 1841 - June 23, 1894

Bessie E. Boulware
wife of George K. Boulware
April 14, 1923 - March 14, 1963

Kendrick E. Smith
November 28, 1913 - June 27, 1960

William I. Jones
August 27, 1866 - April 7, 1929

Ora Lee Durrette
November 28, 1890 - June 23, 1933

Laura Jones Durrette
October 7, 1863 - December 7, 1933

Robert A. Durrette
November 13, 1879 - September 18,
1926

Jane Jones Mullen
March 21, 1854 - October 7, 1903

Alice Jones Skinner
January 27, 1856 - August 21, 1903

Stanfield C. Jones
Co. V, 9 Va. Cav., C.S.A.

Thomas Kirby Boulware
November 24, 1890-November 21, 1948

George W. Boulware
November 3, 1864 - May 13, 1934

Carrie F. Boulware
March 2, 1869 - February 2, 1931

Sherwood White Boulware
January 20, 1889 - October 1, 1958

James A. Cash
Delilah M. Cash
by James A. Cash, Jr.

Three Graves Marked Liberty Church

Mr. Sumner

Mrs. Sumner

Lora E. Long
wife of R.L. Long
January 26, 1886 - December 1, 1920

Willie T. Jeter
wife of S.B. Jeter
April 3, 1868 - March 27, 1924

Samuel B. Jeter
May 5, 1858 - April 27, 1948

George E. Brown
1860-1904

G. Everett Farish
1853-1930

Anna B. Farish
wife of George E. Farish
August 18, 1861 - September 24, 1909

Florence Gertrude Farish
December 28, 1890 - February 13, 1860
George Hazelwood Farish
August 4, 1883 - October 26, 1946

Eola I. Farish
January 1, 1885 - October 11, 1957

Tommie C. Thomas
March 14, 1882 - July 4, 1953
Anna D. Thomas
February 27, 1883 - September 18, 1959

Greenlawn Cemetery

Liza Travillian Loving
1820-1911
Sallie Nelson Loving
1856-1936

Lewis Fitzhugh
son of R.L. & S.K. Brooks
June 27, 1906 - July 20, 1907

Anne Brooks

Harvey Brooks

R.L. Brooks

Henry Carter

William Henry Brooks

Mary Lou Brooks

Mrs. Patton

James Taylor Eubank
November 30, 1843 - August 18, 1930
Entered the Confederate Army, June
1861
Ordained in Ministry, December 1877

Roberta T. Eubank
wife of Rev. J.T. Eubank
May 21, 1852 - October 31, 1928

Roger Dunaway

Leonard Lamar Holloway
August 20, 1906 - May 19, 1931

John Dillard Farish
August 14, 1857 - December 30, 1909
Lelia Holloway Farish
April 11, 1868 - June 11, 1959

Robert Vivian Farish
May 20, 1893 - December 6, 1959
His wife Eloise Early Garth

Infant Sale

Alice Ida Wright
December 5, 1867 - December 16, 1912

W.F. Taylor

Emma Taylor

Bernard R. Clarke
1891-1952

Elizabeth B. Clarke
1868-1951

Clarence T. Clarke
1864-1925

H. Corbin Bowie
October 11, 1899 - July 5, 1955

Walter N. Bowie
December 28, 1893 - January 4, 1962
Lucy V. Bowie
July 18, 1894 -

Infant White

Infant Broaddus

Willie D. Bowie
September 14, 1884 - August 11, 1935

Eugene A. Chewning
November 8, 1910 - January 23, 1961

A. Baynham Broaddus
February 26, 1866 - October 21, 1937

Lucy B. Broaddus
April 28, 1873 - February 11, 1915

Ada Lou Bowie
May 12, 1873 - October 12, 1946

Charles Jesse Bowie
1851-1931

Fannie P. Bowie
May 6, 1859 - Jan. 18, 1904

Greenlawn Cemetery

Eugene Miller Bowie
1879-1885

JESSIE

Nannie Jessie

Julia Irene White
wife of Eugene Bowie
May 31, 1853 - July 24, 1885

Eugene Bowie
March 22, 1854 - December 3, 1910

Sophia Hoomes Corbin
wife of Eugene Bowie
January 12, 1866 - January 30, 1946

Willing Bowie
December 11, 1899-December 26, 1942

Eugene Bowie
June 17, 1891 - August 12, 1940

Ruth Bowie Fondren
June 4, 1893 - February 17, 1952

Louise A. Jeter
May 9, 1892 - August 25, 1904

Jeremiah G. Jeter
February 17, 1856 - November 8, 1910
Bessie W. Jeter
October 6, 1854 - June 9, 1946

J. Jones

Five Graves Marked Liberty Church

George Bullock

Robert Bullock

Jeanie Chinault
mother of Mrs. Lee Bottoms

Ann Eliza Buckner
1832-1887
Married Summerfield Fitzhugh

Summerfield Fitzhugh
Sgt. Co. G, 47 Regt. Va. Vol., C.S.A.
January 29, 1830 - April 9, 1886
Born in Prince William Co., Va.
Died in Caroline Co., Va.

Aylett Hawes Conway
Pvt. Co. B, 9 Reg. Va. Cav., C.S.A.
July 2, 1824 - January 28, 1892

Anne Hawes Conway
1814-1886
Married Dr. Thomas Rowe
of Rowe's Hill

Jacob Edgar Mayo
1861-February 12, 1912
of Albemarle Co., Va.

Frances Katherine Fitzhugh
December 9, 1858 - February 20, 1936
Married A.H. Conway, June 23, 1881
Married J.E. Mayo, June 28, 1896

George Fitzhugh Conway
May 16, 1882 - March 12, 1958
Son of A.H. & F.K. Conway
A Judge of the Craoline County Courts
from April 23, 1923 to March 2, 1958

Fannie Helen Henshaw
July 22, 1888 -
daughter of Ida L. & T.S. Henshaw
wife of George Fitzhugh Conway
Married October 29, 1921

Oric Jones

Jenifer R. Brooks
October 18, 1884 - February 10, 1956

Frank B. Brooks
March 20, 1920 - March 5, 1947

Clement Marshall Harris
November 8, 1864 - August 6, 1922

Maude E. Collawn
wife of Clement M. Harris
April 22, 1875 - August 1, 1950

63

Lottie Collawn
wife of Edgar W. Mills
Born in Caroline County, Virginia
December 7, 1877
Died at Fredericksburg, Virginia
April 14, 1907
Edward Wyatt Mills
March 22, 1874 - January 29, 1908

Sarah Jane Travis
Born in Putnam Co., N.Y.
November 11, 1820
Died at New London, Va.
January 20, 1893
The wife of Dr. A.G. Travis and Mother of
E.B. Travis of Peekskill, N.Y., F.M. Travis
of New London, Va., S.F. Travis of
Cocoa, Fla. and Henrietta Christian of
Peekskill, N.Y.
A Methodist

Dr. A.G. Travis
Born in Putnam Co., N.Y.
December 28, 1818
Died at New London, Va.
November 21, 1885
A Baptist

F.M. Travis
Born November 15, 1849
at Farmers Mills, Putnam Co., N.Y.
Died July 8, 1925
Master of Kilwinning Crosse Lodge
No. 2-237 of A.F. & A.M. in 1894

Bettie Boyd Callawn
wife of F.M. Travis
September 3, 1849 - June 20, 1933

Edna E., wife of Jas. T. Cosby
and daughter of F.M. & B.B. Travis
January 15, 1880 - September 5, 1911

Edgar Callawn

Lottie Collawn

Lelia Pearl, daughter of
William Newton and Virginia E. Collawn
July 8, 1883 - August 19, 1904

Robert Aubrey, only son of
W. Newton & Virginia E. Collawn
August 8, 1880 - Mary 20, 1902

Virginia E. Bradley
wife of Willian Newton Collawn
March 22, 1845 - May 3, 1929

William Newton Collawn
December 21, 1849 - August 4, 1930

Mary B. Gouldin
March 15, 1882 - May 13, 1955
Walker L. Gouldin

Five Buckner Family Graves

Thomas, son of
John and Sarah Buckner

Richard Campbell Buckner
son of John Breckenridge and Allie White
Buckner
October 24, 1889 - January 15, 1963

Henry Aylette Buckner
son of John Breckenridge and Allie White
Buckner
June 6, 1902 - February 10, 1951
[Mason]

John B. Buckner, Sr.
Born June 18, 1856
at Rappahannock Academy, Caroline Co.,
Va.
Died September 23, 1921
Allie W. Buckner
Born January 17, 1865
in Erath County, Texas
Died May 4, 1930

Holloway C. Collawn
January 16, 1888 - December 18, 1920

R.S. Collawn
Co. A, Gant's Bn., Va. Res., C.S.A.

Mollie F. Spindle
wife of R.S. Collawn
November 3, 1845 - May 12, 1914

64

Greenlawn Cemetery

William B. Pitts
1871-1941

Lelia T. Pitts
1872-1953

Katherine Hoover Davis
1905-1953

Charles Stringfellow Hooper, Sr.
1877-1957

Sallie Hudgin Boulware
October 15, 1857
Age 1 yr. & 15 days

Eudora L.
daughter of J.M. & S.P. Bell
January 23, 1888 - June 6, 1904

S.P. Bell
wife of J.M. Bell
March 9, 1855 - September 28, 1909

Lillie H. Thornton
September 6, 1876 - October 2, 1950

Henry F. Thornton
June 22, 1880 - October 9, 1944

Ollie W. Carter
December 19, 1859 - August 6, 1926

Thomas J. Bell
October 16, 1880 - May 16, 1958

Thomas Guy Kay
1886-1961

Cora Bell Kay
1878-1955

Uranie Trice Kay
1849-1916

Robert Allen Kay, Sr.
1848-1920

Burleigh Hamden Kay, Sr.
1880-1936

Eliza A. Pugh
wife of Alexander J. Pugh
July 8, 1942 - December 24, 1916

Alexander J. Pugh
December 11, 1839 - March 22, 1914

Landon C. Boulware
1877-1946

J.W. Collawn
Died January 20, 1897
in his 39th year

Judith S. Collawn
Died June 8, 1879
in her 58th year

W.S. Collawn
Died July 15, 1870
in his 68th year

Walter Scott Collawn
January 9, 1845 - December 3, 1914

Thomas Boughton Collawn
April 1864 - April 12, 1920

Elenora Collawn
March 4, 1852 - May 26, 1927

Frederick E. Collawn
March 4, 1852 - May 26, 1927

Virginia
wife of R.B. Semple
Died in Fredericksburg
February 26, 1944
aged 25 years

W.E. Travis, Jr.
son of Dr. Joseph H. & Eliza Travis
Born July 10, 1855, near Paris, Tenn.,
Died May 19, 1899

Edward Gordon Thornton
son of H.F. & M.S. Thornton
August 19, 1850 - April 4, 1891

Greenlawn Cemetery

William S. Downing
Died February 23, 1848
aged 73 years

Rufus Downing
Died August 2, 1844
aged 61 years

Fanny Downing

John P. Downing
Died November 4, 1856
aged 33 years & 3 mos.

Arlene Virginia Carter
August 10, 1843 - October 2, 1943

Dennis M. Carter
January 24, 1950 - March 24, 1953

Victor B. Carter
May 1, 1907 - August 9, 1959

Three Infants of Lawrence B. & Charlottie
Carter

Lawrence B. Carter
November 27, 1871 - January 13, 1955

Charlottie E. Carter
April 11, 1874 - July 11, 1953

Mrs. Mamie Gallahan Carter
Died November 18, 1862
aged 65 yrs.

Four Unmarked Graves

S.N.T.

William Walker Wiltshire
May 23, 1962
aged 63 years

Mrs. Preston Wiltshire

Preston Wiltshire

Lewis Long

Cornelius Long

Lulie Long

Addie Long

Mrs. Sale

Mr. Sale

Byrd L. Carter
December 1, 1858 - March 30, 1930

Louise B. Thomas
September 15, 1857 - April 7, 1916

Mary B. Skinker
October 25, 1861 - November 18, 1925

John W. Kidd
Va. Pvt. G.D. Det.
29 Inf. Div. W.W. II
January 11, 1916 - May 26, 1954

Richard Allen Sale
May 28, 1848 - January 23, 1926
his wife Lucinda Pugh Sale
February 26, 1871 - December 2, 1960

George Martin

John Martin

SALE

SALE

Julian H. Loving
May 13, 1877 - September 13, 1930
Virgie G. Loving
August 11, 1887 - December 9, 1957

Benjamin L. Carter
Died December 11, 1917

Mittie V. Carter
Died June 6, 1902

66

Greenlawn Cemetery

Russell J. Carter
1889-1958
Annie L. Carter
1902-

Willard Loving

Evelyn Loving

Madge Loving

Lewis Durrell Loving

Lulie Loving

Phillip G. Reynolds
July 31, 1900 - September 23, 1945

Phillip U. Reynolds
July 9, 1869 - March 17, 1948
Lucy E. Reynolds
August 2, 1869 - February 23, 1945

Henry E. Reynolds
March 23, 1910 - July 27, 1953
Carolyn C. Reynolds
April 15, 1914 -

Arthur Lynwood Garrett
1878-1936

Joseph Carl Finkle, infant
December 6, 1930

Lewis F. Goulding
March 29, 1850 - September 14, 1909

Mollie L. Goulding, wife of Lewis F.
October 20, 1848 - January 16, 1926

Charles Andrew Sale
January 22, 1881 - October 1, 1938

Martha Ellen Sale
wife of T.H. Motley
August 31, 1854 - January 6, 1931

Martha Ellen Sale
wife of Edmund Sale
December 1, 1819 - March 22, 1894

Infant Sale

Nannie E. Sale
1850-1901

James Judson Sale
1845-1908

Thomas Hugh Motley
1856-1932

Lizzie Lee Broaddus Motley
1860-1898

Ora Motley

Tommie Motley

Laura Motley

Dr. T.W. Goulding
February 4, 1811 - August 6, 1884

Louisa E. Goulding
December 12, 1817 - June 17, 1896

Dora Dillard Broaddus

Lucy L. Gouldin
wife of John W. Broaddus
October 19, 1842 - August 11, 1889

John W. Broaddus
December 10, 1834 - January 8, 1905

Gouldin L. Broaddus
1881-1955
Mabel P. Broaddus
1885-1952

Mollie Bullock
September 30, 1862 - February 18, 1928

Infant Bullick

Edgar L. Bullock
November 19, 1891 - June 12, 1910

James E. Bullock
December 24, 1860 - June 16, 1924

67

Greenlawn Cemetery

Annie Laura
wife of James E. Bullock
April 4, 1869 - November 15, 1948

John Alfred Skinner
1886-1900

William Presley Skinner
1855-1936

Alice Garrett Skinner
1856-1944

Virginia Gouldin Broaddus
August 6, 1908 - April 27, 1949

Frank Duncan Broaddus
1873-1947

Martha J. Broaddus

William I. Broaddus
September 28, 1811 - July 27, 1874

Thomas R. Goulding
1855-1934
Nannie H. Goulding
1862-1944
Mary G. Goulding
1900-1923

Infant Goulding

Lewis Judson Sale
August 6, 1886 - June 24, 1911

Mary Alma Sale
August 17, 1909 - age 17 yrs.

Infant Sale

Virginia Alice Sale
June 18, 1855 - July 17, 1918

William R. Sale
August 27, 1848 - April 29, 1905

Mary Goulding Skinker
May 29, 1881 - March 29, 1961

William Ernest Skinker
January 28, 1878 - February 23, 1957

Julian Wyatt Garrett
September 27, 1869 - July 27, 1956

Ellen Gouldin Garrett
February 11, 1875 - July 27, 1956

John G. Gouldin
TR, H 9th Va. Cav., C.S.A.
1834-1921

Virginia G. Goulding
wife of John G. Goulding
July 20, 1844 - July 31, 1924

John Herbert Gouldin
July 8, 1881 - February 8, 1950
Frances Pitts Gouldin
March 21, 1888 -

George Walker Sale
1884-1947
Ruth Gouldin Sale
1888-

William Edward Sale
Va. Sgt. Med. Dept., W.W. I
October 25, 1888 - October 15, 1951

Burnley Gouldin Coleman
June 25, 1964 - March 16, 1961

Unmarked Grave
[From A.P. Hill area, 1941]

Sallie T. Marshall

Eugene Broaddus

Polly Saunders

Clarence W. Marshall

Kate Saunders

Carrie Saunders

James Preston Saunders

68

Greenlawn Cemetery

Sallie A. Catlett
wife of C.H. Lefoe
September 27, 1903 - aged 52

Charles H. Lefoe
August 29, 1850 - August 11, 1882

Infant Lefoe

Infant Lefoe

J.H. Lefoe
April 21, 1901
aged 46 years
["Frank" on footstone]

Bettie V. Catlett
wife of J.H. Lefoe
June 9, 1860 - November 2, 1905

Marcus Cash

Oscar L. Cash

Henrietta Cash

Adelia Cash

Bayhnam Cash

Mary Cash

D.S. Cash

Jeanne Cash

Mrs. Sterne

David Sterne

Lucy Sterne

Susan Cash

Oscar Cash

Mary Cash

Mary Sterne

Margaret Annie LeFoe
wife of John W. LeFoe
March 6, 1859 - May 19, 1943

John W. LeFoe
December 14, 1853 - January 12, 1913

George E.
son of John & M.A. LeFoe
September 16, 1879 - October 16, 1881

Nellie B.
daughter of J.H. & B.V. Lefoe
February 27, 1884 - September 22, 1884

Robert H. Gouldin
1893-
Jane P. Gouldin
1894-1958

M. Eulalia Coleman
May 26, 1887 - March 19, 1925

Bethesda Church Grave

Bruce Walker Sale
April 6, 1953 - December 17, 1958

Janet Gay Sale
April 6, 1953 - December 17, 1958

Floyd A. Gouldin
1872-1955
Lillian A. Gouldin
1872-1962

James Ellis Garrett
1841-1901

Emma Smith Gravatt
1845-1900

William Robert Garrett
1876-1896

John James Garrett
1874-1900

69

Greenlawn Cemetery

George Ellis Garrett
July 25, 1884 - August 17, 1955
Susie LeFoe Garrett
September 29, 1884 -

Virginia M. Goulding

J. Frank Goulding
Died September 15, 1897

Susan B. Gouldin

Clarence Goulding

James M. Goulding

Bettie Alice Kidd
December 29, 1847 - February 25, 1929

M. Lou Kidd
December 15, 1840 - November 6, 1891

Lewis T. Kidd
March 3, 1823 - July 21, 1896

William J. Kidd
February 7, 1825 - April 14, 1902

Benjamin F. Kidd
August 19, 1834 - May 4, 1905

Nellie Gouldin Broaddus
March 25, 1857 - February 5, 1921

John Robley Broaddus
husband of Nellie Gouldin
June 17, 1860 - August 14, 1935

Lavinia A. Saunders
November 5, 1838 - November 27, 1922

Julia D. Bullock
April 6, 1893 - June 25, 1954

Walter L. Brooks
July 12, 1897 - January 24, 1962
Mattie LeFoe Brooks
November 13, 1882 - October 23, 1960

Robert Covington

Jane F. Ratcliffe
wife of T.I. Ratcliffe
Died July 10, 1899
in her 45 year

Infant Bullock

Thomas B. Rose
May 20, 1848 - November 26, 1935

Cora Lee Greenstreet
October 29, 1867 - September 30, 1950

L.M. Greenstreet
April 19, 1843 - April 4, 1913

Sallie Broaddus Kidd
May 18, 1843 - October 23, 1905

Thomas Boyd Toombs
1859-1918

Edmonia Gouldin Toombs
1877-1953

Edward Gordon Thornton
1886-1952
Belle Goulding Thornton
1880-

Robert Lewis Garrett
December 5, 1853 - December 6, 1953

James C. Edwards
September 7, 1848 - June 3, 1937

Emma M.
wife of J.C. Edwards
September 15, 1864 - September 1,
1925

Ida Edward Gouldman
May 26, 1897 - May 6, 1920

William H. Edwards
Va. Cpl. 116 Inf., 29 Div. W.W. I
December 19, 1893 - August 18, 1950

70

Greenlawn Cemetery

Nellie Blanch Gatewood
wife of Ula Vincent Blanks
Died May 1, 1934

Laura B. Conway
wife of C.B. Conway
March 3, 1868 - April 18, 1941

William Reynolds

Anne E. Reynolds

Nannie F. Catlett
May 18, 1921, aged 51 yrs.

R.S. Catlett
June 15, 1899, aged 80 yrs.

Catharine A. Lefoe
wife of R.S. Catlett
August 11, 1901, aged 68 years

Willie L. Wright
August 28, 1896 - March 13, 1905

Emma S. Wright
October 8, 1869 - October 26, 1933

W.L. Wright
Co. K, 30 Va. Inf., C.S.A.
1846-1919

Frank T. Catlett
July 20, 1872 - August 3, 1926

Mary Frances Holloway
daughter of R.G. & Joannah Holloway
March 8, 1837 - April 27, 1910

Unmarked Grave

Robert Leland Motley
June 20, 1956
aged 51 yrs. 9 mos. 22 days

Unmarked Grave

Wande Jean [Brooks]
195_

Wirt Taylor Hicks
June 22, 1892 - October 3, 1951

James R. Micou

Marion Micou

Mary Micou

Georgie Micou

David T. Bullock
September 26, 1834 - April 8, 1923

Mary C. Saunders
wife of David T. Bullock
January 26, 1841 - March 15, 1924

Hattie E. Bullock
September 17, 1866 - April 10, 1935

Vernon H. Bullock
July 15, 1878 - May 10, 1961
His sister Ida L. Bullock
January 16, 1873 -

Florence Bullock Clift
April 24, 1863 - October 14, 1942

Jane F. LeFoe
wife of Hiter L. Raines
August 4, 1886 - April 10, 1918

Lawrence H. Raines
May 10, 1882 - October 5, 1922

Two Graves Marked "Ida Bullock"

Levane Ann Holloway

Three Graves Marked "Ida Bullock"

Addison Holloway

Charles A. Holloway

Eliza Bullock

Kate M. Holloway

71

Greenlawn Cemetery

Martha Bullock

Mrs. Allen Rose

Allen Rose
Two Graves Marked "R.A. Bullock"

Two Buckner Infants

In Memory of
Richard Henry Buckner
of "The Neck,"
Born in Caroline County, Va.
Previous to 1760
William Aylette Buckner
Feb. 13, 1766 - June 2, 1830

Mrs. Richard Buckner (wife of Richard
Henry Buckner)

Clarence McKenney
August 22, 1868 - January 5, 1924

Mary J. McKenney
February 18, 1866 - June 5, 1962

Willie McKenney*
July 9, 1877 - March 15, 1942

Fanny G. McKenney
September 26, 1881 - March 8, 1954

Richard H.W. Buckner
Co. B, 9 Va. Cav., C.S.A.

Mollie B. Buckner

Walker Buckner

Mary Smith Buckner
February 2, 1844 - December 14, 1927

Mollie Buckner

Mark Boulware
February 23, 1852 - February 19, 1855

---

*Obituary in The Caroline Progress gives
1952 as death year.

Mark Boulware
October 10, 1846
in his 64th year

Mrs. Lucy Boulware
wife of Mark Boulware
February 25, 1852
in her 70th year

Lucy Jane, daughter of
William Thornley and Sarah P. Boulware
November 11, 1839-November 25, 1845

Mary Alice Jordan
December 12, 1856 - March 20, 1859
Aged 2 yrs. & 3 mos.

W.T. Boulware

Sallie Jordan

Ethel [illegible]

Daniel Rollins
August 29, 1832 - February 23, 1918

Mrs. Daniel Rollins
April 24, 1910, age 86 yrs.

Sallie P. Rollins
May 10, 1862 - July 1, 1931

Alpheus Rollins
October 26, 1874 - June 20, 1926
Fannie Rollins
February 18, 1880 - January 9, 1950

Robert S. Bruce
May 19, 1892 - August 30, 1956

Glassell H. Marshall
1909-1957

Marion Hearn Bruce
August 29, 1888 - October 1, 1962

Samuel B. Hearn
January 28, 1841 - October 9, 1917
Mary V. Hearn
December 12, 1850 - June 26, 1921

Greenlawn Cemetery

William R. Bruce
1873-1946

Mary E. Bruce
wife of William R. Bruce
1873-1950

Julia F. Garrett
wife of R.L. Garrett
Novembr 1831 - November 1912

Infant son of
Charles R. & Hattie W. Bruce
February 22, 1946 - February 24, 1946

Clarence M. Bruce
1902-1906

Charles R. Bruce
1914-1960

Willard T. Boulware

Eva Boulware

Infant son of
Elizabeth B. & Caywood Herndon
March 23, 1935

Charles Francis Myers

Maggie Lee Martin

Gouldie Lee Martin
August 11, 1958
aged 47 yrs. 1 mo. 6 days

Joseph B. Martin
Va. Pvt. Co. B, Inf. Trng. Bn. W.W. II
September 3, 1910 - July 17, 1960

Walker J. Garnett
February 27, 1902 - April 20, 1957

Walker Garnett
December 9, 1873 - June 3, 1946

Sallie Garnett
October 12, 1875 - August 16, 1956

Mrs. Fannie Bruce Garrett
October 22, 1962
aged 65 yrs.

Unmarked Grave

Unmarked Child's Grave

John William Ayers
1878-1926

Unmarked Grave

Dana C. Smith
January 10, 1881 - February 24, 1948

Virginia W. Beazley
June 14, 1886 - June 16, 1946

Robert Penn Beazley
April 28, 1875 - April 11, 1958

Baby Boy Wenige
June 26, 1954

Unmarked Grave

Bagby H. Rouse
1872-1945

Mary E. Rouse
1875-1951

James A. Farmer
December 8, 1869 - February 26, 1945

W.P. Beazley
1911-1955

Two Unmarked Graves

Frank T. Richards
1869-1945
Alice W. Richards
1867-1956

Clara C. Richards
July 13, 1897 - February 8, 1952

73

Greenlawn Cemetery

Chas. W. Seal
June 10, 1878 - May 29, 1948
[Mason]

Irene M. Seal
August 29, 1881 - February 16, 1957

Three Unmarked Graves

Stephen Mercer Brown
January 28, 1900 - April 24, 1953

Gladys B. Watts Carroll
May 11, 1910 - August 25, 1956

Leona Frances Seymour
November 11, 1961
age 44

Aubrey L. Martin
January 26, 1905 - February 2, 1957
Mary Y. Martin

Unmarked Child's Grave

Zelman R. Ramsey
February 6, 1963
aged 75 yrs.

John Wesley Noel
July 15, 1957 - February 13, 1958

Bettie G. Gouldin
1880-1957

Thomas J. Madison
1888-1956

Unmarked Grave

Joseph Allen Young
Age 69

Unmarked Grave

Lucian Franklin Bruce
February 18, 1868 - January 16, 1953

James P. Bruce
1875-1951
Lucy S. Bruce
1896-

Edith Pugh Payne
January 6, 1915 - August 10, 1962

Malvonia W. Collawn
1876-1951
Ena Watts Collawn
1884-1958

Sarah Ellen Epting
1877-1958

Wilson Jerome Epting
1871-1951

G. Leslie Pitts
April 8, 1905 - February 22, 1947
Gladys D. Pitts
October 30, 1905 -

Robert Woolfolk
October 7, 1876 - February 10, 1952

Frank E. Bruce
1876-1942

Unmarked Grave

C.L. Buchanan
March 17, 1890 - December 6, 1956

Charles Fowler Gamble
Va. S.F.C., U.S.A., W.W. II
July 28, 1912 - November 9, 1955

Bernard K. Allen
July 19, 1916 - April 19, 1955

Harry Franklin Pitts
August 20, 1916 - July 28, 1953

James Robert Pitts
December 24, 1904 - August 11, 1957

Greenlawn Cemetery

David L. Bruce
1890-1957
Nannie S. Bruce
1901-1952

Floyd Stevens Smith
September 15, 1888 - August 7, 1952

Charlie B. Pitts
1877-1954
Effie B. Pitts
1882-1951

Chastian F. Collins, Jr.
May 3, 1884 - October 7, 1948

John J. Blanton
October 26, 1899 - November 4, 1953

Unmarked Grave

Ashton Bert Brooks
son of Page and Emma Brooks
Va. P.F.C., Hq. Co.
Armd. Repl. Tng. Cen. W.W. II
December 24, 1923 - July 6, 1957

Unmarked Grave

Paige Hunter Brooks
January 30, 1962
aged 76 yrs.

John Humphrey Brooks
December 13, 1962
aged 83 yrs.

Philip H. Chinault
June 13, 1935 - October 20, 1954

John Franklin Chinault
February 22, 1889 - November 5, 1955
Emma Loving Chinault
August 24, 1903 -

Clarence E. Brooks
1880-1955

Lottie B. Brooks
1887-1950

Robbie Baylor Parr
December 31, 1878 - January 13, 1956

Marcie Watts Parr
May 6, 1879 - July 4, 1956

Clifton James Carneal
December 1, 1931 - August 17, 1955

Julian B. Parr
July 6, 1924 - October 16, 1960

Herbert L. Parr
January 28, 1914 - May 3, 1955

Irvin F. Brooks
1904-1904
Gladys I. Brooks
1907-1908
Julian W. Brooks
1920-1920

Emma Flippo
September 18, 1894-December 18, 1921

Edward J. Flippo
May 26, 1888 - December 3, 1933

Thomas J. Flippo
January 24, 1858 - April 29, 1946
Mary Ella Flippo
December 8, 1864 - Janaury 5, 1932

Mary Ella Flippo
wife of Lawrence B. Durrett
May 5, 1891 - November 29, 1918

Douglas W.
infant son of D.C. & Lillian Jones
May 21, 1949 - June 23, 1949

Felix Winston Campbell
May 29, 1913 - June 28, 1957

David Lee Martin
July 6, 1942 - March 29, 1962

John Randolph Martin
December 8, 1942 - September 22, 1962

Greenlawn Cemetery

Harry Kenneth Beazley
April 8, 1917 - August 1, 1939

Harry L. Beazley
October 22, 1882 -
Bessie F. Beazley
September 19, 1892 - December 7, 1956

Alger Earl George
April 27, 1896 - December 19, 1960

Charles B. Collins
June 17, 1907 - February 14, 1959

Alfred R. Reynolds
April 12, 1891 - May 3, 1962
Annie P. Reynolds
July 18, 1894 -

Stuart R. Acors
September 17, 1925 - August 4, 1957
Va. P.F.C., Co. H. 273 Inf. Regt.
W.W. II, B.S.M.

Grace K. Pugh
August 16, 1888 - September 4, 1960
Henry C. Pugh
January 26, 1885 -

Ernest L. Upshaw
Va. P.F.C., Co. B 318 Inf.
W.W. I, P.H.
October 22, 1894 - October 24, 1960

Maurice Sylvia
December 15, 1888-December 31, 1960

Everette B. Allen
June 22, 1899 - July 22, 1956

Dellie Catlett Carter
1881-1962

Albert Carter
Va. P.F.C., 1114 Svc. Comd. Unit
W.W. II
July 27, 1912 - September 9, 1957

Mary C. Edwards
December 25, 1877-November 30, 1957

Richard Beazley
1881-1962
Rosa Belle Beazley
1889-

Arthur Farmer
January 8, 1897 - July 30, 1961
Lula M. Farmer
May 3, 1899 - January 1, 1961

James E. Lumpkin
March 5, 1877 - January 25, 1958
Mary C. Lumpkin
September 11, 1881 - August 16, 1961

Frank T. Selph
June 19, 1944 - June 23, 1944
Stuart K. Selph
October 19, 1957 - February 20, 1958

Thomas Milton Gouldin, Jr.
April 27, 1918 - August 24, 1958

Weyman Ralph Selph
May 10, 1923 - May 26, 1958

Perry E. Madison
June 6, 1907 - March 2, 1959
Kate S. Madison
November 26, 1906 -

Lal A. Brown
August 30, 1884 - August 17, 1959

Ora Whittaker Brown
1893-1939

John M. Stevens
May 13, 1887 - August 26, 1960

John William Bigelow
February 15, 1886 - December 12, 1958
Mina Starks Bigelow
May 12, 1888 - July 18, 1961

John B. Beazley
August 18, 1877 - February 14, 1958
Ocie C. Beazley
July 14, 1887 -

Greenlawn Cemetery

Andrew J. Wright
September 17, 1892 -
Lucy L. Wright
December 18, 1888-September 29, 1957

Mrs. Cora Lee Whittaker
July 10, 1962
aged 79 yrs.

John Herbert Farmer
1877-1958

Unmarked Grave

William Webb McDonald
January 1, 1959
aged 47 years

Unmarked Grave

Mrs. Thompson

Mary N. Sale

John H. Crowell
June 21, 1915 - March 8, 1954

Fannie Selph
Died at the age of 92 years

Woodrow W. Brown
February 14, 1914 - November 4, 1958

Robert Skinner

Mary Skinner

Charlie Skinner

Jannie Skinner

Infant Skinner

J.M. Heflin

Ivey Dillon

Ben Carneal

Janie Heflin
1887-
Minor Heflin
1888-1946

Shirley Heflin
1933-1936

Peggy Heflin

Vernon Heflin
1914-1947

HEFLIN

Helen Heflin

HEFLIN

A.L. Wright

William Wright

Thomas Riddle

Betty Riddle

Katie Riddle

Tom Riddle

John Baptist Wright

Sallie Post

Elizabeth Riddle Claytor

Two Handmade Stones

Betty Jane Anderson

Unmarked Grave

William Riddle

John Riddle

Maria Riddle

Rosemon Riddle

77

Greenlawn Cemetery

Kate Riddle

Loulie Jane Samuel Anderson

Mary E. Mould
1886-1961

Champ Chinault
1860-1861

Lucy Chinault
1881-1886

Salome Chinault
1864-1871

Andrew B. Vaughan
1891-1894

Infant Chinault

Infant Chinault

Infant Chinault

Eddie Chinault

Infant Chinault

Arthur C. Chinault
1846-1911
Bessie E. Chinault
1875-1900

Sarah A. Chinault
1850-1904

Louisa A. Chinault

Garnett Chinault

Jesse M. Chinault
1884-
Florence R. Chinault
1883-1951

Mrs. Dewey Jordan

Seven Garrett Family Graves

Jennis E. Garrett
March 20, 1888
age 3 yrs.

Two Andrews Family Graves

Six Unmarked Graves

Three Graves Marked by Handmade Stone

J.H.J.
Died April 20, 1930

Frank Samuels
June 22, 1880 - February 23, 1937

Percy E. Samuels, Jr.
Born and Died April 20, 1934

Wayland Samuels
September 7, 1918 - February 27, 1919

C. Victoria Samuels
July 20, 1944 - April 11, 1945

Bromly N. Jordan
September 16, 1884-November 18, 1921

Neaty T. Farmer
February 24, 1880 - August 19, 1920

Jeff D. Jordan
January 8, 1908 - February 4, 1932

Marle Jordan
May 8, 1915 - October 1, 1915

Myfee Jordan
June 14, 1909 - May 6, 1918

Secous E. Jordan
September 13, 1924-September 17,
1924

Steven Jordan
July 5, 1912 - July 14, 1913

Littleman Jordan
March 20, 1911 - May 6, 1918

78

Greenlawn Cemetery

Charles W. Jordan
September 18, 1917 - November 8, 1918

Willie F. Loving
April 9, 1881 - June 15, 1948
Kanawha F. Loving
January 12, 1879 - February 1, 1943

Orsey Ann Farmer
November 10, 1865-December 20, 1866

Four Graves Marked "Lloyd Farmer"

Russell Farmer
Va. P.F.C., 101 Inf., 26 Inf.
Div. W.W. II, B.S.M. & O.L.C. - P.H.
February 23, 1917 - June 30, 1956

Thomas Farmer
January 18, 1871 - March 30, 1944

Irvin Jordan

A. Jones

Sarah Taylor

Christopher Columbus Taylor
1847-1922

Charlie O. Loving*
April 27, 1901 - September 11, 1938
Cassie S. Loving
April 23, 1906 - June 22, 1950

Frances A. Jones
1866-1929

Irvin S. Farmer
July 24, 1881 - May 22, 1904

Cora Bell Farmer
July 6, 1856 - November 24, 1922

John Y. Farmer
October 26, 1857 - September 23, 1928

L.S. Jones
November 11, 1917
age 11 yrs.
A.M. Jones
November 16, 1917
age 9 yrs.

Nicodemus Jones, Sr.
1875-1945
Fendie Wheeley Jones
1879-1962

Willie C. Wheeley
April 4, 1869 - September 1, 1951

John L. Elliott
March 15, 1844 - July 10, 1904
Nannie M. Elliott
August 28, 1870 - December 14, 1899

Charlie Bruce

John Bruce

Eva Bruce

Nine Bruce Infants

Charles H. Rouse
December 5, 1960
age 76 yrs.

Mary Anderson Sylvia
April 8, 1873 - February 3, 1947

Sylvia
died 1956

Mary Walker Rouse
April 12, 1952
aged 84 yrs. 6 mos. 10 days

---

*Obituary in The Caroline Progress gives
death date September 11, 1939, age 37.

79

Greenlawn Cemetery

Lucian Jordan
May 12, 1870 - November 21, 1945

Elizabeth T. Jordan
June 28, 1880 - February 23, 1953

Herman Richard Jordan
April 18, 1963
age 56 yrs. 3 mos. 22 days

Two Graves Marked "J.P. Bruce"

Susan Noll

Salis Bruce

Sarah F. Bruce

Bettie L. Houston
May 7, 1870 - December 23, 1922

Julia Samuel

Charlie Wheeley

Lucian Wheeley

Nannie Wheeley

William Wheeley

Four Unmarked Graves

Kellis Infant

Minnie Lumpkin

Lumpkin Infant

Lumpkin Infant

Farmer Infant

Ben Loving

Susan Farmer
1854-1922

Eugene Farmer
1850-1933

Charles C. Garrett
January 3, 1885 - November 22, 1918

Robert H. Watts
June 6, 1904 - December 15, 1933

Mary Carter

Lucy Wright

Robert Wright

Susan B. Wright

Lulie B. Wright

James H. Wright
Thornton's Co. Va. Lt. Arty, C.S.A.

Sarah F. Wright
June 6, 1850 - December 5, 1923

Mattie Wilson Garnett

Two Graves Marked "James H. Wright"

Ridgely Lumpkin

Dorothy Lumpkin

Hannah Wright

Otis Wright

Junior Wright

L.C. Wright

Robert L. Taylor
Co. H., 30 Va. Inf., C.S.A.

Phebe J. Taylor

J.W.R. Taylor

Belle P. Taylor

R.L.T. Taylor

Greenlawn Cemetery

Richard B. Wright
February 25, 1954
age 72

Mrs. Elizabeth Wright
September 22, 1956
age 77

Two Unmarked Granite Stones

Grave With Unmarked Handmade Stone

TRICE

Etta Lumpkin

Bessie Lumpkin

Blanche Lumpkin

John Lumpkin

COATES

LUMPKIN

Alice Chinault

Luvinia Lumpkin
October 14, 1835 - August 14, 1912

George Lumpkin

Farmer Infant

Unmarked Graves

C.L. Toombs
December 17, 1958
age 83

Deloach Infant
November 30, 1961

William Joseph Collins*
Sept. 9, 1902 - May 11, 1962

Florence Kidd Hite*
Died Jan. 19, 1957

---

*Graves moved from the Collins Family
Cemetery at "Hickory Grove" near Penola,
Virginia.

Site of Hopewell Christian Church

Originally located at the present intersection of Route 601 (Penola Road) and Route 207, on the site now occupied by Feedlot Restaurant. Hopewell Christian Church was organized on September 30, 1887, by 22 former members of nearby Emmaus Christian Church who had significant concern over the issue of drinking. The founding members included: B.C. Burnett, Sr., Pam Burnett, B.C. Burnett, Jr., Angelina Burnett, Mignonette Burnett, John J. Blanton, Sarah E. Diggs, Ellen Ophelia Diggs, Josie Lumpkin, Sallie Lumpkin, Archibald Blanton, John T. Blanton, Ann Blanton, Sallie Haley, Ada Burruss, Ann Marmaduke, George Marmaduke, Mary Marmaduke, and Atwill Cannon.

After the building burned, the congregation disbanded. A small cemetery existed near the church, but there were no tombstones. One might suspect that some of the individuals named above may have been buried here. The remains of these graves were moved across the road in 1968, when Route 207 (now Rogers Clark Boulevard) was widened into a dual highway through this area.

The graves are now in a wooded area. The road enters into the woods a few yards after one turns right off the Penola Road on to Route 207, heading toward Bowling Green, Virginia.

Hopewell Methodist Church

Located at the intersection of routes 606 and 607, at Guinea, Virginia. Hopewell Methodist Church had its beginning on October 27, 1867, when Edgar McKenney deeded land for the purpose of building a church. The structure became a part of the Caroline County Circuit in 1870. Shortly thereafter in 1876, T.J. Bayton became minister of the Bowling Green Methodist Circuit which included Hopewell, Bowling Green and Shiloh churches.

This church converted from oil lights to electricity in 1940. The building has changed very little in style, and has a neat pristine look of a rural country church. The early leaders of the church included the families of Catlett, Garnett, Gray, and Martin. Ministers have included Rev. T.J. Bayton, R.O. Payne, E.L. Peerman, and Benjamin F. Holstein, Jr.

This site was visited on September 23, 1961.

L.O. Lucy
1951
"Luch"

B.F. Mills
1858-1922

Emma Mills
1861-1936

Mercer A. Nunn
May 11, 1859 - Jul. 29, 1912

Mollie Walter Nunn
Jul. 14, 1861 - Jan. 10, 1926

Myers A. Munn
1918-1945

Bessie F. Dabney
Mar. 24, 1859 - Dec. 14, 1922

Charles Curtis Dabney
son of C.B. and Bettie Durrett Dabney
June 9, 1865 - Jan. 8, 1943

Eva Lucy Dabney
1861-1948

J. Mercer
son of Carroll and Blanche Hazzard
Aug. 28, 1916 - Dec. 22, 1929

Charlotte A. Cosby
Aug. 17, 1841
Jan. 9, 1886

Napoleon D. Cosby
Jan. 3, 1826
June 4, 1894

Lillian W. Thomas
1898-1925

83

Lakewood Cemetery

The earliest recorded tombstone in this cemetery was for William Lewis Maury in 1878. In the Acts of the Virginia Assembly, 1889-1890, page 625, is found the act to incorporate the Bowling Green Cemetery Company. The capital stock was not to be less than $200 nor more than $2,000, and shares were to sell for $10 each. Dr. C.S. Webb, John G. Rowe, George R. Collins, A.B. Chandler, and William T. Chandler were the trustees. Each lot sold included eight grave sites.

Lakewood cemetery is located on Lakewood Road in Bowling Green, Virginia. It is found by turning left off Broaddus Avenue, just east of the intersection of routes 301 and 2. Proceed on Lakewood .4 mile to Broaddus' Mill Pond. The cemetery is on the left side of the road and on top of the hill from the pond. The plat of this cemetery is kept by Storke's Funeral Home of Bowling Green, Virginia.

This site was visited in 1962.

Valentine Fitzhugh Makeley
1860-1945

Henry Lewis Washington
February 24, 1869 - December 18, 1950

Grace Coghill Washington
Octber 19, 1882 - January 18, 1944

Henry Washington, Jr.
December 24, 1912 - June 28, 1960

Vernon Drewery Lucy, Sr.
June 25, 1925 - age 82 yrs.

Cora Lee Toombs
September 20, 1894 -
Albert Owen Toombs
Va. E.M.I. U.S.N.R., W.W. II
October 24, 1920 - November 28, 1961

Unmarked Grave

Floyd F. Beasley
1899-1940

Scenia W. Beazley
April 22, 1861 - June 10, 1940

Luther S. Beazley
September 28, 1854-December 23, 1939

Jesse Lee Toombs, Sr.
June 25, 1961, age 77 yrs.

Ernest Lee Toombs
September 5, 1912 - October 27, 1937

Mildred B. Andrews
October 23, 1936 - January 30, 1937

Louise K. Andrews
1886-1935

Cecil B. Andrews
1870-1948

Leroy Martin
1915-1944

John W. Simpkins
May 15, 1857 - June 6, 1936
Catherine E. Simpkins
August 10, 1865 - June 17, 1936

Sadie E. Whittaker
November 28, 1904-September 25, 1939

84

Lakewood Cemetery

William J. Whittaker
May 28, 1872 - February 4, 1947

Alice L. Satterwhite Noel
August 2, 1893 - August 13, 1962

John H. Noel, Jr.
July 28, 1915 - September 1, 1944

Meta Huger Flegenheimer
July 11, 1958

John W. Satterwhite
December 16, 1937 - March 22, 1949

Oscar Satterwhite
Va. Pvt. 1 Cl., 318 Inf. 80 Div.
February 21, 1936

Lawrence E. Martin
1882-1947

Lucy Ann Paytes
May 9, 1899
June 13, 1951

Four Unmarked Graves

Walter Levi Munday
Apr. 9, 1875 - July 19, 1955

Mrs. Parke Taylor Mundie
February 7, 1963
age 84 years

Charles H. Kidwell
December 10, 1904 - February 13, 1960

Joseph W. Sorrell
June 5, 1871 - August 13, 1951

Molly T. Sorrell
July 23, 1876 - June 27, 1957

Mamie Withers Brown
Nofember 25, 1900-September 18, 1957

Julian E. Carter
Apr. 26, 1932 - Apr. 15, 1935

R.R. Henderson
1883-1955

Blanche Taylor Henderson
1883-1962

Lawrence Earl Southworth
1895-1951

Bernice L. Gatewood
December 6, 1920 - March 25, 1936

J.H. Gatewood
1866-
Mattie L. Gatewood
1875-1900

General W. Gatewood
September 2, 1896-December 22, 1917

Infants of J.H. & Mattie L. Gatewood
1900

Miss Emma Carr Gatewood
June 31, 1963
age 92 years

Nannie Winston Gravatt
August 10, 1872 - August 25, 1961

Walter Hazelwood Gravatt, Sr.
January 6, 1854 - December 2, 1936

Walter Hazelwood Gravatt, Jr.
October 2, 1901 - October 14, 1949

B.A. Dratt
June 21, 1876 - January 29, 1936

Susie B. Gatewood
September 20, 1882 - January 31, 1956

Jean M. Pitts
July 9, 1933 - June 7, 1937

Lakewood Cemetery

John Dillard Green
Lieutenant, Army of U.S.
Born July 13, 1913 - Killed at Stadtkyll,
Germany, March 6, 1945
Buried at Foy, Belgium. Moved to Henri
Chapelle, Belgium.
3rd Army, 87th Div.

Elizabeth Kish
1866-1950

Stephen Kish
1861-1936

Anna Kish
1878-1946

Infant son of Evert B. & Virginia B. Puller

Evert Battle Puller
October 3, 1903 - August 22, 1948

William D. Jerrell
June 28, 1877 - June 9, 1950

Sallie D. Jerrell
February 28, 1886 - October 19, 1929

George Fell
1877-1956

Willie Fell
1875-1949

Robert L. Smith
1867-1929

Elizabeth A. Fell
1871-1932

William Riter Carter
September 28, 1862-December 25, 1932

Imogene Hearn Carter
June 29, 1871 - October 13, 1957

Ashton Carlyle Carter
August 24, 1890 - September 4, 1933

Mattie Garrett Barlow
September 30, 1884 - March 13, 1949

Bessie Dillard Travis
September 1, 1891-November 10, 1935

Roscoe C. Travis
February 2, 1887 - March 23, 1943

Sallie B. Grimes
1864-1936

Andrew Lee Boulware
November 2, 1896 - October 21, 1949

Edward Coulter Stehl
February 9, 1951 - November 17, 1952

Jack H. Crowell
Va. Pvt. 337 Inf. W.W. II
May 24, 1907 - October 27, 1951

Unmarked Grave

Leslie Albert Bodine
July 29, 1872 - July 8, 1952

Albert Norman Bodine
83rd Div. 1st Army
Capt. U.S. Army
Born September 2, 1914 - Killed in action
July 5, 1944
Buried St. Laurent, France

Graham Henderson Powers
1902-1953

Wilbur Russell Broaddus
May 16, 1873 - May 9, 1951
Pauline Garman Broaddus
November 28, 1883 -

Eugene Beauharnais Travis
October 12, 1876 - June 22, 1958
Maud Broaddus Travis
July 26, 1878 - January 24, 1951

Lakewood Cemetery

George Harold Crawford
Major U.S. Army, C.A.C.
Husband of Helen Satterlee Travis
Born Fairfield, Washington, Dec. 15, 1908
Graduated U.S. Mil. Acad. Class 1933
Captured at Correigidor P.I., May 7, 1942
Killed in Subic Bay P.I., December 15, 1944

Walter Wilson
July 7, 1863 - March 20, 1945

Our Baby

William MacConnell
September 22, 1897 - October 18, 1947

Minnie Brooks Coleman
1880-1944

Minnie L. Coleman
1881-1944

Ernest L. Brooks
January 12, 1932

Nannie C. Brooks
wife of Ellis M. Brooks
November 19, 1925

Ellis M. Brooks
March 5, 1855 - August 9, 1932

George W. Gray
October 3, 1860 - October 30, 1942
Sallie P. Gray
June 12, 1865 - June 19, 1945

Chauncey Gray
October 17, 1834 - December 14, 1917
Mary A. Gray
June 12, 1837 - December 17, 1917

Wilbert Chauncey Gray
January 30, 1894 - December 30, 1960

John D. Gray
1861-1929

Jacob Ditzler
Born January 13, 1831, Oldham Co. Ky.
Died March 29, 1918 at Milford, Va.
Florence Howell Ditzler
Born October 30, 1850, Montgomery Co. Ky.
Died April 27, 1918 at Clarendon, Virginia

Everett L. Beazley
September 19, 1872 - December 9, 1921
Evelyn L. Beazley
November 27, 1878 - January 17, 1947

Robert Sym Beazley
October 17, 1951
age 43 yrs. 5 mos. 20 days

Hugh C. Beazley
August 17, 1915 - February 27, 1952

Robert Esmont Whittaker
Va. Pvt. U.S. Marine Corps
November 20, 1926

Two Unmarked Graves

J. Jackson Wright
November 27, 1862 - October 6, 1936
Kate Gray Wright
April 3, 1886 - January 19, 1953

Willie R. Carter
1894 - September 2, 1943
Va. Pvt. 1 Cl. Q.M. Corps
Velma W. Carter
1896-

Rev. Amos Clary
1870-1938
His wife Julia Wharton Jackson
1885-1947

John Randolph Jackson
1850-1939
His wife Elizabeth Wharton
1866-1939

Lakewood Cemetery

Mary Emily Davis
1871-1943

Andrew Broaddus Marshall
1860-1930
His wife Betty Chinn Davis
1867-1955

Dr. Robley Dunglison Bates, Sr.
son of Dr. Thomas J. & Rosalie Lumpkin
Bates
1875-1954
Annie Davis Bates
daughter of George Stapleton and Fannie
Crittenden Davis

Anna Maude Davis
June 25, 1873 - July 13, 1950

Grover C. Bruce
December 25, 1883 - April 16, 1958
Estelle W. Bruce
February 24, 1891 - Mar. 19, 1967

J.H. Whittaker
1854-1937

J.W. Battlestone
1871-1934

G.T. Holt
Died 1945

Vivian E. Thomas
October 2, 1881 - January 12, 1945
Minnie M. Thomas
April 21, 1886 - October 16, 1957

French C. Thomas
November 20, 1854 - May 28, 1960
His wife Garria O. Thomas
November 3, 1858 - October 8, 1936

Everette L. Thomas
September 25, 1905 - August 13, 1937

John C. Liverman
Va. Chief Mach. Mate, U.S.N.R.F.
December 11, 1896 - January 26, 1945

Unmarked Grave

D. Samuel Elliott*
1865-1924

Mary C. Elliott
August 5, 1855 - April 4, 1931

Emmett W. Elliott
1890-1918

Ashby D. Elliott
1873-1950

James S.L. Barlow
1836-1925
His wife Cassandra E.
1841-1918

Lelia Walton Barlow
Jan. 11, 1865 - Dec. 28, 1958

Woody L. Barlow
May 5, 1878 - March 9, 1958

Hillie W. Barlow
Feb. 6, 1876 - Oct. 11, 1952

B.B.**
L.J.B.
S.F.
J.L.B.
C.E.B.

Carrie
daughter of Jno. & Ada Tuma
Age 18 yrs.

Floyd Whittaker
January 15, 1895 - October 16, 1950

Ada Evelyn Whittaker
1920-1920
Mary Elizabeth Whittaker
1918-1921

_____

*Obituary in The Caroline Progress gives
1938 as death year.
**Bradford Barlow, 2½ year old son of
Woody Barlow, died of pneumonia in
January 1923.

Lakewood Cemetery

Frank Linwood Whittaker
February 14, 1922 - February 19, 1922

Frank Whittaker
May 10, 1888 - August 4, 1961
Lula B. Whittaker
March 27, 1896 -

James Sample Brooks
October 29, 1876 - November 23, 1954
Florence Pitts Brooks
June 1, 1878 - February 19, 1961

Florence E. Sullivan
May 11, 1933 - October 31, 1934

Betty Anne Spayd
July 29, 1946 - August 4, 1946

William T. Garrett
March 23, 1867 - October 1, 1946

Ida A. Garrett
Dec. 31, 1868 - July 11, 1949

William F. Dunnington
February 22, 1865 - June 18, 1947

Rosa A. Dunnington
October 11, 1869 - March 16, 1953

Ella M. LePrade
1866-1947

Ethel M. Leathem
1913-1951

Johnny M. Duffer
Va. E.M. 3, U.S. Navy
April 18, 1938 - December 19, 1959

Two Unmarked Graves

Grave Marked With Cross

Luther H. Martin
March 7, 1896 - September 26, 1952

Ernest B. Martin
October 26, 1922 - March 19, 1940

Johnnie Goodwin
April 29, 1943
age 52 years

Unmarked Grave

Strother W. Lewis
Va. Elec. 2 C, U.S. Navy, W.W. I
January 20, 1895 - March 12, 1947

Joseph W. Sale
1880-1940

Laura Gray Sale
February 2, 1962
age 88

Cecil Everett Borkey
April 29, 1894 - August 21, 1951

Joseph Baker
1859-1938

Carroll H. Carneal
May 9, 1927 - January 15, 1950

Perry Irving Carneal
January 22, 1924 - September 9, 1940

Willie Frank Carneal
November 3, 1921 - August 30, 1939

Laura Bell Carneal
January 20, 1877 - August 30, 1940

Eugene T. Carter
1926-1941

Samuel T. Carter
1874-1940
Virginia S. Carter
1883-1956

Robert Ridgeway Carter
May 10, 1907
Jan. 13, 1969

Lakewood Cemetery

Myrtle Parker Taylor
January 7, 1914 -
Andrew Haynes Taylor
February 6, 1889 - May 4, 1956

Pitman A. Thomas
1859-1941
Lucy H. Thomas
1866-1942

Clyde A. Clendennen, Jr.
January 6, 1927 - March 7, 1962
Indiana, Sgt. U.S. Army, W.W. II

Father
Joe Hickman Carter
1865-1939

George Ridgely Dorsey
November 18, 1872 - February 13, 1961

Stella M. Shuman
wife of George R. Dorsey
February 8, 1881 - February 7, 1935

George Porter Lyon
1865-1933

Ada Lyon Evans
1867-1953

LYON / HARDING

W.P. Carneal, Jr.
October 13, 1870 - December 21, 1933

Robert E. Acors
June 20, 1892 - January 25, 1955

Frances Chandlee
wife of Edward Ney Dodson
May 26, 1877 - June 17, 1957

William Woodson Broaddus
January 11, 1861 - April 6, 1938
Alice Motley Broaddus
October 14, 1873 - January 9, 1956

Charles Baynham Mahon
July 25, 1869 - May 12, 1952

Cora Carter Mahon
August 16, 1866 - August 6, 1943

Infant son of J.J. & F.A. Cain
1909

John J. Cain
December 18, 1864 - December 26, 1941

Florence A. Cain
July 4, 1868 - November 10, 1946

Edmund Lee Henshaw
January 27, 1896 - December 26, 1955

Edna Carter Henshaw
October 13, 1898 - June 16, 1959

Martha Frances Henshaw
wife of Goodloe Gooch
April 5, 1861 - August 7, 1940
daughter of Thomas P. Gatewood
Henshaw & Virginia O. Scott Porter

Thomas Scott Henshaw
son of Thomas P.G. Henshaw & Virginia
O.S. Porter
December 8, 1857 - April 3, 1907
Married December 17, 1884 to
Ida Lee Henshaw
daughter of Thomas Elmore Henshaw and
Sarah Ella Tod
December 4, 1864 - December 31, 1936

Twin Infant Daughters of
Ida Lee & T. Scott Henshaw
May 6, 1900 - May 6 & 20, 1900

Tod Scott Henshaw
October 21, 1898 - October 10, 1949

Bernard Webb Mahon
June 14, 1898 - March 25, 1961

Peggy Mahon
August 7, 1927 - November 13, 1927

James T. Richards
November 2, 1863 - January 2, 1925

90

Lakewood Cemetery

Nettie Rowe Richards
August 6, 1874 - March 12, 1926

Thomas E. Barlow
1870-1951

Della L. Barlow
1867-1925

Maurice B. Taylor
October 1885 - January 1959

William B. Madison
February 1864 - March 1940

Carrie T. Madison
December 1876 - January 1958

Lucy E. Taylor
December 1850 - January 1909

Muscoe L. Taylor
January 1851 - February 1929

Susie Haynes Taylor
June 1875 - January 1955

Eloise E. Taylor
Died July 2, 1923

Wilson N. Blatt
March 28, 1881 - July 30, 1923

Rosa Wagner Blatt
January 20, 1871 - August 30, 1943

J.A. Blatt
May 1, 1891 - November 8, 1951

Wm. George Taliaferro
1861-1944

Fannie F. Taliaferro
1868-1926

Simeon B. Overton
Minister of the Gospel
1867-1942

Margaret Sawyer
wife of S.B. Overton
1865-1931

C.W. Coghill
July 25, 1870 - September 2, 1940

C.S. Coghill
January 27, 1872 - July 2, 1941

E.S. Coghill
January 3, 1875 - January 19, 1953

E.R. Coghill
November 17, 1842-November 15, 1925

B.K. Coghill
February 23, 1843 - May 16, 1924

Pattie S. Farish
October 13, 1861 - July 7, 1956

William Pettus Miller
November 30, 1870 - March 14, 1953

Annette Ditzler Miller
June 24, 1878 - December 8, 1941

John G. Pavey
Thornton's Co., Va. L. Arty., C.S.A.

James W. Barlow
June 22, 1858 - January 7, 1935

Carrie Frank Barlow
December 3, 1866 - November 7, 1948

John S. Frank
January 2, 1836 - October 28, 1881

Lucy Ellen Frank
May 11, 1846 - September 4, 1923

Mrs. Martha Taliaferro Broaddus
January 19, 1963
age 72 yrs.

91

Lakewood Cemetery

William Boulware Broaddus
son of Dr. William Lee & Kate Garnett
Broaddus
December 7, 1872 - November 10, 1923

John Garnett Broaddus, M.D.
son of William Lee Broaddus, M.D. and
Kate Garnett Broaddus
February 10, 1881 - September 19, 1951

W. Emma Lear Broaddus
daughter of William Wilkinson Lear and
May Nolley Lear
November 16, 1884-November 19, 1951

Alice Mildred Broaddus
Died June 12, 1958

Mary Muscoe Broaddus
Va. 1st Lt. Army Nurse Corps
W.W. I & II
January 4, 1962

Kate Garnett Broaddus*
April 21, 1850 - July 16, 1926

William Lee Broaddus
January 30, 1846 - January 4, 1914

Caroline Garnett Broaddus

Anne Winslow Broaddus
Died February 7, 1952

F. Susie White Hickman
1883-1916

Angelina E. Mundy White
1846-1928**

Laura Carneale White
1881-1962

Tall Pointed Stone Without Inscription

M. Louise Haines
June 15, 1890 - June 20, 1958

Alice W. Haines
April 16, 1856 - August 3, 1955

Joel Haines
January 16, 1837 - August 22, 1917

Robert S. Wright
December 26, 1879 - March 23, 1958

Robert A. Parr
1861-1936
Rosa C. Parr
1861-1918
Kate A. Campbell
1855-1945
Joseph R. Campbell
1858-1947
Nannie P. Wall
1902-1953

Mary Chewning Wright
Died January 16, 1944

Jennetta Collins Chewning
Died September 6, 1917

Louis Carlton Garrett
September 19, 1874-November 16, 1955

Clarence Wyatt Garrett
April 18, 1869 - May 7, 1954

Margaret Jones Garrett
Pvt. Co. F, 3 Regt. Va. Inf., C.S.A.
March 10, 1837 - October 9, 1916

Margaret Shepherd Webb
1889-1952

Charles S. Webb, M.D.
April 10, 1846 - November 28, 1935

May Camper Webb
wife of Charles Shepherd Webb
1870-1957

---

*Obituary in The Caroline Progress gives
July 15 as death date.
**Obituary in The Caroline Progress gives
birth year 1845 and death date January 4,
1928, at age 83.

92

Lakewood Cemetery

Caroline Webb Cundiff
1828-1917

Catherine Webb McCurdy
1836-1911

Garnett Lewis Martin
wife of Dr. William C. Webb
1908-1943

Robert Henry Webb
Virginia
S. Sgt. 97 Bomb G.P. A.A.F.
World War II, A.M. & 90 L.C.
April 29, 1909 - July 20, 1961

Judith Ann Ennis
1845-1931

Lilah Croshaw Ennis
1849-1915

Geo. Aylette Thornton
1852-1911

Ella T. Chewning
1862-1938

William S. Chewning
1863-1911

Charles T. Jesse
October 19, 1878 - September 15, 1960

C. Ridgely Jesse
1911-1912

Joseph Edmund Jesse
1872-1934

Sarah Annie Jesse
1846-1920

Peter T. Jesse
1881-1919

Laura
daughter of G.F. & K.W. Pugh
April 24, 1911 - April 12, 1912

Gustavous F. Pugh
July 22, 1879 - October 27, 1956
Kate W. Pugh
February 1, 1877 - January 14, 1941

Arthur R. Williams
January 15, 1903 - October 17, 1857

Edgar B. Collins
May 21, 1860 - March 19, 1941
Florence B. Collins
April 7, 1860 - January 6, 1941

Margaret Collins Webb
June 18, 1884 - March 3, 1947

Edna Earle Collins Webb
January 1910 - July 1911

Sadie B. Martens
1879-1953

George Blythe
Age 25 years

Aubrey Garrett
1883-1962

Mary B. Garrett
1889-1962

Winston Garrett
1910-1944

Carrie Blythe Foster
Died April 1938

Benjamin G. Blythe
January 16, 1913
age 71 years

Leroy Pugh
March 19, 1888 - March 27, 1960

Benjamin McC. Pugh
March 3, 1890 - March 22, 1911

Betty A. Pugh
1858-1946

Lakewood Cemetery

R.L. Pugh
December 29, 1861 - June 14, 1930

Julia E. Stiff
June 5, 1842 - July 21, 1886

James Hampden Stiff
March 29, 1885
age 54 yrs.

T.H. Stiff
1861-1920
his wife C.W. Stiff
1860-1935

Mary Elizabeth Payne
September 29, 1910
aged 71 yrs.

Mary Eliza Sutton
1857-1910

Aaron Burton Sutton
1853-1936

David Clarence Glascock
Mar. 7, 1889 - Oct. 20, 1963

Jane Bertrand Collins
wife of David Clarence Glascock
June 15, 1894 - Nov. 17, 1963

George Todd Collins
Va. Pvt. Btry. C, 110 Field Arty., W.W. I
March 9, 1882 - October 4, 1956

Julian Hart Pitts
December 19, 1874 - April 4, 1932
Bertie Pugh Pitts
February 24, 1868 - August 16, 1944

Richard F. Potts
1916-1930

Julian M. Bruce
1857-1936
Etta L. Bruce
1875-1941

Two Infants of Alfred Bruce

Beale P. Southworth
May 12, 1914 - March 12, 1931

Columbia L. Loving
October 17, 1857 - June 18, 1939

Annie P. Southworth
March 30, 1895 - June 15, 1950

Emily Louise Flanders Maury
March 17, 1873 - May 7, 1928

Charles Walker Maury
November 23, 1858 - October 24, 1935

William Lewis Maury
Lt. U.S.N., Capt. C.S.N.
1813-1878
Anne Fountaine Maury
1832-1890
Children
William Lewis Maury
1858-1879
Charles Walker Maury
1858-1935
Harriet Woolfolk Maury
1860-1861
Leonard Turner Maury
1863-1904
Rutson Maury, M.D.
1865-1892
Henry Tobin Maury
1867-1926

1853 William Buchanan 1925
1859 Virginia Wilson Maddox Buchanan
1925
1888 Charles Hall Maddox Buchanan
1908
1891 Gideon B. Buchanan 1925
1883 William Thomas Buchanan 1883 -
buried in West Grove Cemetery,
Harrison Co., Ohio

Charles Harris Taylor
April 20, 1877 - May 9, 1934

Infant Daughter of Blanch & C.H. Taylor

94

Lakewood Cemetery

Frank B. Borkey
March 25, 1858 - April 26, 1943

Sarah S. Borkey
June 1, 1865 - May 12, 1927

William C. Chapman
August 17, 1886 - March 4, 1959

Ida B. Brooks
1863-1926

William G. Brooks
March 6, 1871 - May 10, 1928

Belle Hampton Collins
wife of Elwood D. Davies, Jr.
December 19, 1886 - March 21, 1954

R.E. Collins
June 18, 1850 - March 18, 1925

Belle Burke Collins
May 7, 1857 - August 18, 1924

E. Burke Collins
September 16, 1877 - June 12, 1938

Pearl C. Collins
April 23, 1888 - December 31, 1949

George Waverley Collins
February 11, 1882 - May 13, 1960

Thomas Orin Hyatt
October 29, 1881 - June 14, 1955
Sadie Collins Hyatt
April 8, 1880 - November 21, 1957

Mervin E. Elliott
March 30, 1888 - December 24, 1956

Bessie P. Elliott
April 5, 1890 - February 2, 1930

John W. Elliott
1859-1941

Ida Belle Elliott
1860-1938

John William Elliott, Jr.
Va. 2 Lt., Coast Arty. Corps
December 10, 1937

Russell J. Elliott
June 30, 1894 - May 24, 1952

Lloyd Bransford Elliott, Jr.
February 4, 1963
aged 41 years

Dorothy Priestley
daughter of L. Bransford & Dorothy Elliott
January 6, 1919 - June 2, 1926
[(Miss Boo) on footstone]

Dorothy Priestley Elliott
June 9, 1899 - October 2, 1946

Lloyd Bransford Elliott
Va. Apprentice Seaman, U.S.N.R.F.
January 16, 1897 - Jan. 22, 1944

Richard M. Gray, Jr.
April 1, 1906 - January 12, 1958

[illegible] Hammond
Died 1953

R.M. Gray
October 1868 - April 14, 1921
Nettie P. Gray
wife of Richard M. Gray
December 18, 1872 - October 10, 1953
["Bessie" on footstone]

Elizabeth G. Carneal
May 18, 1843 - February 3, 1925*

W.P. Carneal**
January 23, 1844 - April 16, 1905

Robert W. Carneal
March 10, 1875 - August 9, 1943

---

*Obituary in The Caroline Progress gives
February 4 as date of death.
**Moved from Zoar Baptist Church in Fort
A.P. Hill by Jack Davis in 1942.

95

Lakewood Cemetery

Porter D. Caldwell
Va. Pvt. Essex Cavalry, C.S.A.
October 10, 1846 - February 4, 1925

Ann Williams Caldwell
November 5, 1846 - August 25, 1920

MARTIN
Gracie Bruce
1892-1859
Will Irvin
1892-

W.L. Bruce
November 15, 1855-September 22, 1928
age 73 yrs.

R.S. Bruce*
July 20, 1850 - January 20, 1928
age 74

Unmarked Grave

William D. Beazley
August 20, 1888 - December 3, 1955

Vivian B. Puller
March 18, 1907 - October 18, 1959

Emmett C. Puller
October 11, 1911 - August 13, 1925

Ella N. Broaddus
February 28, 1858 - April 19, 1921

Melville T. Broaddus
October 19, 1857 - May 2, 1935

Eugenia W. Gravatt
February 16, 1921 - August 29, 1921

Mary Emma Gravatt
March 29, 1963
age 86 years

Lillie Ann Gravatt
February 26, 1873 - September 3, 1960

Kate May Gravatt
January 29, 1880 - January 5, 1960

Mary Jane Gravatt
March 23, 1844 - October 15, 1927

Robert S. Gravatt
May 23, 1841 - May 7, 1916

Harry Gregory Moore
August 3, 1866 - March 31, 1919
his wife Annie James Wright
February 15, 1873 - September 28, 1959

Rena Belle Wright
dau. of James & Mary Susan Wright
January 1, 1868 - March 15, 1946

Mother
Mary S. Wright
1842-1918

Edythe Thelma Elliott
Daughter of Mr. & Mrs. Robert Elliott
Born July 22, 1902
Died July 15, 1906

George William Beale
Capt. 4137 Strategic W.G.
A.F. Korea A.M. & 2 O.L.C.
January 9, 1927 - March 30, 1961

Richard Lee Beale
1882-1928

Louisa Brown Glassell
1856-1953

Russell William Glassell

Andrew McMellan Glassell, M.D.

Frances Downing Glassell

Fanny Ware Glassell

John Downing Glassell

---

*Obituary in The Caroline Progress gives
death date for Robert "Bob" Bruce as
January 20, 1924, aged 75.

96

Lakewood Cemetery

William Downing Glassell

Andrew McMellan Glassell, C.E.

Ada Glassell

Mary Eugenia Glassell

Robert Taylor Glassell, M.D.

Marion Glassell
wife of Percy H. Walker
Died October 11, 1905

Inez Rixey Deaner
January 6, 1881 - January 6, 1911

Lizzie L. Rixey
April 21, 1858 - June 28, 1913

James W. Rixey
August 25, 1846 - December 23, 1908

Irene C. Morris
Nov. 2, 1882 - Jan. 5, 1829
[note error]

Irene Rixey
June 8, 1850 - April 27, 1910

Thomas C. Rixey
December 22, 1847 - October 20, 1909

Mary E. Rixey
April 12, 1816 - July 20, 1907

Mary F. Rixey
February 14, 1853 - May 9, 1936

Sallie F. Bullard
December 27, 1939
age 75 yrs.

Charles R. Bullard
1860-1941
Helen R. Bullard
1875-1934

Edward Everett Butler, D.D.S.
1855-1949

Ora G. Butler
1856-1930

Edward E. Butler
Va. Chief Yeoman, U.S.N.R.E.
January 31, 1941

Ann E. Butler
1836-1919

Travis Bagby
1838-1907

Annie B. Wright
September 15, 1870 - August 2, 1957

Burton L. Wright
December 16, 1858-November 22, 1924

James L. Elliott
1856-1908

Rosa C. Elliott
1854-1929

William Lynwood Elliott
1883-1961

Waverley Elliott
1881-1959

Frances Olivia
daughter of Jane Beckham & James T.
White
December 31, 1838 - April 28, 1910

John Cary
son of John Lewis and Elfie Cary White
October 21, 1882 - January 25, 1949

Elfie Cary White
wife of John Lewis White & daughter of
John B. & Columbia H. Cary
September 3, 1853 - February 19, 1930

John Lewis White
son of Jas. T. & Finnella S. White
April 5, 1848 - April 15, 1916

97

Lakewood Cemetery

Leiper Moore Robinson
of Chelsea, King William County, Va.
October 17, 1845 - September 9, 1910
Co. H, 9th Va. Cavalry, C.S.A.

Unmarked Grave

Herman D. Covington
May 26, 1896 - November 22, 1931
Son, Bernard W. Covington
January 12, 1914 - April 11, 1950

James B. Acors
1870-1914

Mary E. Acors
1873-1962

Chas. H. Loving
August 7, 1855 - March 11, 1939

B.T. Spindle
September 11, 1910
age 58 yrs.

R.H. Pugh
1853-1910

Lewis K. Farish
August 19, 1913
age 33 yrs.

FARISH
Alice S.
1842-unknown
Keeling Row
1839-1910
Catherine R.
1838-1910

Thomas Skinner
Co. H 47 Va. Inf., C.S.A.

Esther Dunn Metcalf
February 6, 1879 - February 20, 1956

Mary Caffrey Dunn
February 21, 1856 - July 4, 1942

E.L.R. Dunn
June 4, 1854 - December 24, 1909

Unmarked Grave

Garland Danwich Carter
Va. Sgt. 24 Ord. Co. (MM)
July 7, 1895 - June 19, 1942

William Buckner Carter
March 31, 1955
age 86 yrs.
[1868-1955 on new stone]

Minnie Margaret Carter
1872-1911

Maggie Carter
October 31, 1911 - July 25, 1912

James Hampton Carter
1900-1928

Ellen Barlow Jones
June 22, 1862 - September 3, 1904
[moved from Mt. Hermon Baptist Church]

Alex. L. Jones
March 17, 1856 - January 26, 1889
[moved from Bowling Green Methodist
Church]

Bettie L. Collins
September 18, 1855 - June 26, 1952

John R. Chandler
March 17, 1903 - June 11, 1923
Elizabeth L. Chandler
December 30, 1904 - December 3, 1912
Charles L. Collins
1864-1921
C. Ridgely Collins
1875-1906
W. Garnett Collins
1898-1899
Edmund P. Sutton
1818-1900

Mary E. Nottingham
July 16, 1857 - January 27, 1906

Smith S. Nottingham
October 13, 1814 - May 22, 1898
Margaret C. Jameson
wife of Smith S. Nottingham
November 19, 1822 - April 3, 1897

Victoria Ayers
1884-1954

Father
Willie P. Ayers
Oct. 3, 1855
April 14, 1939

Lena Sorrell
1862-1930

Laura J. Skinker
wife of B.M. Skinker
May 13, 1873 - October 17, 1919

Ben M. Skinker
1865-1941

The Memory of The People Who Were
Interred in Tudor Hall Cemetery, King and
Queen County, Virginia
Lovel Pierce Tod
February 2, 1809-1880
Fanny Spindle Tod
March 3, 1812-1885
Sarah Ella Tod Henshaw
1837 - November 4, 1908
Their Daughter
Fanny Helen Henshaw
September 18, 1860 - May 21, 1881
Lucy Ann Henshaw
1841 - April 3, 1908
Phillip Elmore Henshaw
August 17, 1885 - October 5, 1885
Robert Edward Henshaw
June 30, 1887 - September 21, 1887
Edmund Scott Henshaw
April 10, 1892 - July 7, 1892

Mollie Tod Bates
1861-1929

Virginia Bird Tod
November 8, 1850 - October 14, 1905

Columbia Tod
September 7, 1848 - September 7, 1896

Jas. R. Collins
son of G.R. & R.J. Collins
August 1, 1870 - July 5, 1901

E. Athol Collins
January 12, 1884 - May 19, 1952

Rebecca J. Coleman
wife of Geo. R. Collins
August 1, 1849 - February 8, 1919

Geo. R. Collins
October 10, 1843 - June 22, 1918

Richard G. Moncure
December 24, 1871 - January 27, 1908

Annie Elizabeth Moncure
June 9, 1907 - April 2, 1913

Maria M. Moore
1865-1947

Wayland Brooke Williams
Sept. 3, 1873
Jan. 31, 1952

Lucy Moncure Gill
1869-1927

T. Benjamin Gill
1858-1928

Eustace Conway Moncure
February 6, 1836 - July 7, 1921

Fanny Irby Moncure
November 7, 1836 - May 26, 1923

Unmarked Lot

Lakewood Cemetery

Norman C. Scripture
1834-1916
Margaret G. Scripture
1874-1923
Mason G. Scripture
1863-1947
Violet S. Scripture
1838-1914

Perry Russell Smoot
September 19, 1891 - June 25, 1892
[duplicate]

Perry Russell Smoot
September 19, 1891 - June 25, 1892
Earl Ryan Smoot
July 20, 1893 - September 26, 1894
Sallie Hill Smoot
wife of Otho P. Smoot
Died March 11, 1898
Also Infant Son
Otho P. Smoot
December 14, 1862 - January 13, 1928

Edward Bagby Smoot
Va. Lt. (J.G.) U.S.N.R., W.W. II
May 31, 1909 - November 21, 1958

P.M. Mills
February 7, 1882 - January 4, 1921

Infant Son of E.V. & P.M. Mills

Bertha Kathleen Vincent
November 20, 1891 - July 11, 1892

Willie Lee Vincent
August 25, 1880 - February 22, 1881

F.B.V.
April 23, 1861 - August 1, 1923

R.D.V.
March 25, 1850 - August 27, 1920

Sallie Roper Rains
wife of William W. Rains
April 30, 1852 - June 8, 1932

William W. Rains
1840-1914

Cordie W. Moncure Rains
January 19, 1878 - June 12, 1945

Roper Rains
January 29, 1886 - March 12, 1956

John Lawrence Jordan
Co. B, 9th Va. Cavalry
June 22, 1846 - December 27, 1924
His wife
Sallie Winston Woolfolk
May 25, 1856 - March 21, 1934

A.P. Gouldman
July 25, 1823 - July 1, 1900

Mary Ellen Gouldman
November 5, 1828 - February 12, 1900

Henrietta G. Gouldman
March 12, 1849 - December 14, 1913

Susan Gouldman
September 7, 1851 - October 7, 1931

William Temple Chandler
Mary 24, 1868 - December 9, 1882

Charles C. Chandler
September 22, 1883 - January 28, 1900

Landon S. and Lucy A. Chandler
February 26, 1888

Howard Raymond Carlton, Jr.
January 22, 1911 - January 29, 1938

Howard R. Carlton
December 3, 1887 - June 24, 1916
[Woodmen of the World]

Lucy A. Chandler
April 4, 1802 - May 5, 1896

John W. Chandler
January 8, 1872 - October 18, 1920

Lakewood Cemetery

A.B. Chandler, Sr.
August 16, 1843 - April 13, 1928

Julia Yates Chandler
February 15, 1847 - November 21, 1934

A.B. Chandler, Jr.
May 12, 1870 - September 20, 1928

Algernon S. French
November 10, 1899 - March 30, 1913

F.W. Chandler
September 19, 1876-December 31, 1907

Cecil Lee Baker
September 24, 1861 - January 3. 1921

Linda Allen Baker
November 22, 1862 - July 1, 1926

Catharine H. Saunders
1805-1893
Addie Saunders Pittman
1834-1909
Richard H. Saunders
Co. C, 47 Regt. Va. Inf., C.S.A.
1836-1910
Thomas W. Valentine
1824-1901
Mollie Saunders Valentine, his wife
1840-1898
Catherine Pearl Valentine
infant dau. of Thomas C. & Pearl
Valentine
February 23, 1902
Aubrey Valentine
1870-1924
Pearl H. Valentine
wife of Thomas C. Valentine
1884-1938
Thomas C. Valentine
1868-1949

Unmarked Lot

Robert Hudgin
son of Wescom Hudgin & Ellen Hardia
Clerk of Circuit and County Courts of
Caroline, 65 years
April 24, 1892
aged 90 yrs.
Capt. Jack Hudgin
son of Robert Hudgin & Sally Graham
February 4, 1899
aged 60 yrs.
Represented his country in the House of
Delegates of Virginia

Webb R. Davis
1895-1919

John P. Davis
1859-1946

Mary E. Davis
1875-1912

Mrs. Leverne Getrost Davis
September 10, 1962
age 58 yrs.
[1903-1962 on new stone]

Bessie G. Davis
February 23, 1894 - October 13, 1894

Conway Gay Davis
1897-1901

Mary Garrett
January 22, 1893

Mary Louise Garrett
1896-1954

Maria Lou
wife of M.G. Garrett
1857-1933

Montgomery G. Garrett
1857-1938

William H. Pugh
May 26, 1854 - March 8, 1937

Lakewood Cemetery

Christina E. Pugh
March 1, 1857 - March 7, 1937

William W. Pugh
October 24, 1883 - April 25, 1884

Mary E. Eubanks
1828-1893

Eugene Gordon Allen
April 11, 1903 - July 12, 1903

Eugene G. Allen
1856-1917

Lillian Harris Allen
November 26, 1868-December 17, 1952

Martha Ruth Barlow
wife of Arthur H. Allen
July 2, 1890 - October 25, 1956

Anna Wenrich
March 14, 1889 - March 4, 1890

Father Wenrich
October 9, 1842 - October 31, 1901

Mother Wenrich
January 10, 1857 - October 11, 1901

Daniel Wenrich
August 22, 1878 - August 26, 1903

Samuel Wenrich
December 30, 1891 - April 17, 1922

Lillie Hilliard Ennis
wife of William E. Ennis
September 24, 1867 - January 7, 1900
age 32 yrs.
William Edwin Ennis
1863-1915

J.G.E.

Lelia Morris Downing
1860-1934
John Pendleton Downing
1856-1939

James Ashby Ennis
November 8, 1875 - March 20, 1934

Carroll C. Ennis
1870-1941

Overton "Otie" Woodward Ennis
January 5, 1868 - January 16, 1950

Bertha Ennis Burruss
March 19, 1873 - March 11, 1959

Jack M. Ennis
October 4, 1875 - August 28, 1891

Father
Joseph L. Selph
1907-1935

Annie E. Beazley
Nov. 7, 1903
Aug. 13, 1918

Lily Gray Kay
October 20, 1866 - August 7, 1935

Carroll Edwin Kay
1st Sgt. Co. C, 116 Inf. W.W. I
Died in France
February 4, 1919
age 27 yrs.

Columbia R. Ennis
1837-1913

James Edmund Ennis
October 4, 1898
age 67 yrs.

Arthur S. Samuel
July 11, 1830 - January 10, 1909

Hardenia Samuel
October 25, 1933 - July 13, 1910

Julia Samuel
January 16, 1940

102

Lakewood Cemetery

William C. Digges, C.V.
Co. B, 9th Va. Cav.
Died January 31, 1918
age 73 yrs. 2 mos.

William E. Frazier
November 2, 1872 - September 27, 1923

Two Unmarked Graves

Everett Edgar McKenney
October 17, 1827 - October 12, 1873

James Lindsey Coleman
October 23, 1839 - July 7, 1889

Jacob Luther Farmer
November 3, 1838

Annie E. Beazley
November 7, 1903

Richard Bagby Broaddus
December 12, 1871 - January 19, 1957
Madalaine Throm Broaddus
January 2, 1874 - June 13, 1954

Virgie M. Pickett
1885-1915

Elizabeth Whittaker
1863-1918

Thomas J. Whittaker
1861-1936

Edwin L. Poats
May 23, 1922 - June 6, 1928

Harry C. Poats
June 25, 1874 - January 19, 1958
Addie A. Poats
August 30, 1890 - December 26, 1953

Lewis L. Poats
1841-1917
Laura A. Poats
1848-1931

Benjamin Franklin Smoot, Jr.
1870-1941

Florence Rowe Smoot
July 16, 1868 - January 27, 1954

Benjamin Smoot

Clara Bernice Meyer
1882-1960

Jacob Bond Meyers
December 5, 1878 - April 18, 1959

Martha E. Walker
wife of J.H. Meyer
August 5, 1845 - January 1, 1914

John Henry Meyer
December 15, 1845 - May 16, 1918

Bertha Meyer Bruce
December 13, 1880 - October 7, 1960

Blanche M. Wright
1875-1958

R.E. Wright
1866-1926

Ernest G. Smoot
1878-1954
his wife
Eva Nelson
1878-1945
Lillian M. Smoot
May 6, 1903 - November 2, 1906
Doris Grey Smoot
April 17, 1923 - October 23, 1924

Oscar Gresham
Co. H, 9 Va. Cavalry, C.S.A.
February 12, 1836 - March 1, 1914
C.T. Gresham
July 3, 1841 - September 11, 1905

In memory of my wife
Catherine Taliaferro Gresham
Born July 2, 1842
married Oct. 26, 1882
Died Sept. 11, 1905
[duplicate; differs]

Charlotte [Gresham]

Charles [Gresham]

William Wallace Wright
August 14, 1847 - January 1, 1936
Annie Davies Wright
August 7, 1850 - March 18, 1937

Jane C. Wright
1827-1911

William Wright
1818-1896

Charles E. Wright
July 12, 1882 - August 9, 1951

Charles E. Wright, Jr.
Va. Sgt, 485 A.A.F. Base Unit
December 29, 1916 - May 28, 1946

Joseph S. Davies
Born at Milford, Delaware
June 1, 1823
Died at Bowling Green, Va.
February 1, 1895

Mary Hudson Davies
November 10, 1820-September 23, 1912

Dellie G. Davies
December 5, 1859 - November 30, 1954
Addie G. Davies
December 5, 1859 - November 20, 1954

C.F. Coleman
1835-1891

Unmarked Grave

John Dudley Hudson
Va. Sp. 3, Svc. Co. 26 Inf., 1 Inf. Div.
January 11, 1933 - June 2, 1960

William W. Saunders
Co. F, 30 Regt. Va. Vol., C.S.A.
1845-1903
Sallie S. Hansford, his wife
1848-1913
Richard G. Hansford, their son
1883-1905

Frances H. Rowe
February 4, 1878 - September 7, 1961

Edgar H. Rowe
September 17, 1857 - April 7, 1927

Margaret Ann Rowe
wife of Rev. John G. Rowe
January 18, 1831 - May 26, 1914

John Gallatin
son of Edgar H. & Mary W. Rowe
October 26, 1893 - June 10, 1895

M.W.R. [Rowe]

John [Rowe]

Winslow [Rowe]

A.A. Anderson
1847-1910

M.L. Anderson
1851-1926

A.R. Anderson
1874-1933

Emma Anderson Hite
1885-1955

Charles A. Hite
1887-1937

Margaret Anderson
1880-1896

104

Lakewood Cemetery

Walter Hite
1923-1926

Baby Hite
1919

Robert T. Chewning
August 19, 1855 - April 21, 1898

Daniel Webster Beazlie
April 9, 1858 - December 12, 1912
Elizabeth Throm Beazlie
September 4, 1865 - February 25, 1952
Gustave H. Throm
Mary A. Throm
Mary E. Throm

Mary B. Haymes
Oct. 1, 1890
Mar. 6, 1930

Robert Olin Peatross
June 8, 1835 - November 29, 1905

Mary Elizabeth Peatross
June 4, 1851 - March 2, 1919

James A. Chapman
April 1, 1891

S.W. Broaddus
1842-1923
Emma D., his wife
1850-1883
Emily L., his wife
1850-1923
Carrie M. Broaddus
1883-1894

C.W.B.
E.L.B.

Blanche Ennis Broaddus
March 19, 1873 - January 2, 1957

Eugene Broaddus
January 4, 1872 - March 26, 1960

Charles A. Broaddus
November 14, 1876-September 10, 1961

Ethel Newbill
wife of Charles A. Broaddus
Died June 21, 1958

Thomas Dallas Coghill
August 23, 1844 - April 18, 1924
Mary Campbell Coghill
April 7, 1845 - February 3, 1920

Robert A. Coghill
January 26, 1875 - March 9, 1958

Annie Winston Coghill
June 11, 1875 - October 2, 1952

Rosa Coghill
August 9, 1869 - July 29, 1894

William Timothy Chandler
May 17, 1832 - January 7, 1901
Alice Scott Chandler
August 31, 1842 - June 27, 1904

H.B. Coghill
December 18, 1881 - June 5, 1910

William G. Coghill
1849-1928
Lou L. Coghill
1859-1944

Mary Jane
wife of W.N. Covington
May 1, 1834 - March 18, 1898

Annie E. Covington
June 7, 1862 - October 21, 1939

Mary Elizabeth Covington
August 2, 1856 - October 29, 1927

William Butler Covington
August 18, 1855 - December 31, 1928

John W. Gill
1874-1936

Cora C. Gill
1879-1955

Lakewood Cemetery

Myrtle Winston
wife of L.T. Wright
February 5, 1867 - December 25, 1915

Lulie T. Wright
May 22, 1859 - February 21, 1906

Elizabeth P. Wright
July 25, 1940

Ida P. Brooks Parr
May 6, 1862 - March 21, 1927

Sallie G. Proctor
January 15, 1833 - September 17, 1906

Proctor
1933 - age 91

George W. Trice
March 31, 1856 - January 7, 1930
Alice B.
Feb. 5, 1858 - Jan. 7, 1930

Unmarked Lot

Thomas C. Chandler
March 15, 1840 - March 22, 1919

Mrs. T.C. Chandler
September 11, 1841-December 22, 1902

Two Unmarked Graves

Rebecca Bondurant
Infant daughter of
Ned & Bessie Campbell
Apr. 22, 1916
May 4, 1916

CAMPBELL
Bessie B. Smith
Mar. 27, 1881
Apr. 8, 1970
Thomas Edward
Aug. 5, 1876
Sept. 13, 1937

BEAZLEY
Haywood W.
1875-1948
Mary M.
1889-1939

Raymond Luther Beazley
Feb. 1, 1924

BRUCE
Ruby C.
1885-1947
Brewer V.
1887-1963

Four Graves: Ella Henshaw, Infant
Henshaw, Infant Cain and W.P. Carneal,
Sr., were moved from Camp A.P. Hill area
to Lakewood Cemetery in 1942.

Lebanon Christian Church

Lebanon Christian Church

Located at the intersection of routes 605 and 632, at Welch, Virginia. This church, now known as Lebanon Pentecostal Tabernacle, was organized in 1840. Reverend Albert R. Flippo donated an acre of ground for the church, and was subsequently ordained there. Besides here association with Caroline County, Mr. Flippo was a minister at churches in Hanover, King William, and Louisa counties until his death in 1888. After the decline and decease of many of its founding members, the congregation had by 1900 ceased meeting.

Following the use of the building by the Christian Church, it was used for a while by a denomination known as the Apostolics. Afterward, the County used the structure as a school. The adjacent cemetery seems to be more closely associated with the Pentecostal congregation which later occupied the premises.

This site was visited September 23, 1961.

Frank Wawruszack
Died Apr. 28, 1961
Age 86

Chas. W. McAllister
Died Nov. 10, 1913

Joseph Opalka Wrabets
1875-1951
Age 76 yrs.

John Gacek
1859-1950

Samuel Gogoff
Apr. 15, 1889 - May 26, 1959

Mary S. Gogoff
Dec. 12, 1895 - Feb. 12, 1944

Johanna Kohut
1881-1953
Age 72 yrs.

Mary Llora
Feb. 12, 1914 - Jul. 13, 1944

Mrs. Suzanne Mary Sverchek
Died Aug. 17, 1948
Age 79 yrs.

Mother Susanne Sverchek
1869-1948
[duplicate]

John Sverchek
Died Apr. 29, 1949
Age 78 yrs.

Father
John Sverchek
1871-1949
[duplicate]

George Bobrovsky
Nov. 15, 1884 - Oct. 14, 1954
Age 70 yrs.

Johanna K. Bobrovsky
May 18, 1883 - Mar. 1, 1960
Age 76 yrs.

Mount Herman Baptist Church

Mount Hermon Baptist Church

Located .5 mile below Shumansville, Virginia, on Route 627. Mount Hermon Baptist Church was organized June 11, 1869, after members first met as Union Sunday School in a building next to Shuman's Store. In 1871, a building was erected on the west side of the road from the present building, and completed the next year. This site is today marked by the graves of Grace Taylor and George Allport in the front, and Thomas Chiles and Lewis Lee Sirles in the back. The old frame construction building was rectangular and had two separate entrances on the front, each with a shingle door.

A new church that was erected across the road from the old building was dedicated in October 1898. The former structure fell into disrepair and, after the roof caved in, was finally demolished to make room for a cemetery.

Members here included the Shuman family who came from Germany to Alexandria, Virginia where they founded Shuman's Bakery. The bakery is still in business today. A son, Charles A. Shuman, while traveling through Caroline County on a cattle buying trip, stopped at the home of the Page family, and fell in love with Mr. Page's daughter Olivia. Shuman returned to Caroline County, married Olivia, and settled on a part of the Oakley Farm which was later known as the community of Shumansville. The Shuman and Allport families intermarried and were among the first buried at Mount Hermon. A window that commemorates C.A. Shuman is found in the church.

This site was visited April 23, 1962.

Emmet L. Young
Mar. 5, 1913 - Apr. 21, 1913

Thomas G. Puller
Jul. 7, 1866 - Jan. 7, 1929

Emma V. Puller
Jul. 30, 1871 - Jun. 10, 1934

POLLARD
William L.K.
Mar. 6, 1862 - Aug. 9, 1917
Alice L.
May 26, 1867 - Feb. 7, 1946

Our Mother
Elizabeth Gray
Apr. 27, 1837 - Aug. 4, 1913

Baby Taylor
Son of Frank M. & Hausie W. Taylor
Born & Died Oct. 2, 1928

Mother
Mollie Barlow Pitts
Oct. 21, 1868 - Mar. 4, 1941

Father
Fernando H. Pitts
Nov. 4, 1873 - Jul. 8, 1956

Our Son
Pvt. Harry M. Taylor
Co. C, 126th Inf.
Aug. 24, 1895 - Oct. 12, 1918

Frank L. Taylor
May 18, 1866 - May 22, 1947

Annie B. Taylor
Oct. 6, 1870 - Apr. 7, 1945

110

Mount Hermon Baptist Church

Lucy Ann Chiles Sirles
Nov. 4, 1871 - Jun. 30, 1938

Lewis Lee Sirles
Feb. 7, 1867 - Aug. 22, 1923

Freddie G. Sirles
Virginia Seaman 2 Cl., U.S.N.R.F.
Oct. 12, 1932

Thomas Chiles
Thornton's Co., Va. Lt. Arty.
C.S.A.

Charlie C. Chiles
Virginia Pvt. 109 M.G.B.N.
28 Div.
Dec. 11, 1885 - Oct. 26, 1946

Baby Barlow
May 10, 1924

Joseph A. Barlow
Jul. 14, 1878 - Feb. 22, 1950

Robert Lee Garnett
Feb. 15, 1882 -

Myrtle Mary Garnett
Feb. 13, 1892 - Jul. 6, 1956

Aubrey P. Garnett
Aug. 13, 1922 - May 17, 1955

Walter F. Seal
May 20, 1894 - Jul. 17, 1953

Elizabeth L. Seal
May 16, 1898 - Oct. 1, 1956

GARNETT
Isabell S.
1869-1950
Smedley
1878-1949

Father
Charles E. Brownley
1887-1947

James Francis Healey
Virginia
Cpl. Btry. E, 38 Arty. Cac.
World War I
Aug. 10, 1895 - Mar. 20, 1959
[duplicate]

James Francis Healey
Aug. 10, 1895 - Mar. 20, 1959
Lucy Pearl Cecil Healey
Jul. 27, 1917 -
Luther Calvin Cecil
Oct. 1, 1915 - June 3, 1944

Archie Houston
Co. B, 2 Va. Inf.
Sp. Am. War

TAYLOR
James R.
1874-1937
Susie B.
1890-1958

Lester E. Taylor
Dec. 7, 1924 - June 20, 1928

Carroll Floyd Pitts
Virginia Fl., U.S. Navy
World War I
Mar. 11, 1896 - Nov. 14, 1955

Little Ellen
Lucy Ellen Chenault
Sept. 6, 1921 - Apr. 14, 1954

CHENAULT
W.F.
Husband
M.B.
Wife

Our Darling
Dwite Cecil
son of W.F. & M.B. Chenault
Jan. 21, 1927 - Dec. 26, 1930

111

GREEN
Theophilus R.
July 31, 1873 - Mar. 31, 1936
Mabel A.
Apr. 30, 1868 - Nov. 2, 1935

William Herbert Covington
Feb. 27, 1911 - Sept. 26, 1917

Ernest Evans Brault
Apr. 17, 1948 - Apr. 19, 1948
Alice Lee Brault
Aug. 8, 1950

James W. Southworth
Apr. 4, 1858 - Jan. 22, 1927

Our Mother
Annie Lee Vaughan Southworth
Jul. 3, 1873 - Mar. 28, 1949

Travers Southworth
Oct. 13, 1899 - Oct. 30, 1902

Leonard S. Southworth
Virginia Pvt. Medical Department
World War I
Oct. 19, 1891 - Mar. 27, 1960

Maud Vaughan Thompson
Sept. 26, 1876 - Mar. 28, 1897

James Vaughan
Oct. 8, 1841 - June 16, 1904

Lucy Blanton Vaughan
Oct. 7, 1848 - Aug. 11, 1917

Emeline Blanton
wife of Capt. James Blanton
Dec. 10, 1822 - June 12, 1909

Mrs. Mamie Dyson Vaughan
Died May 31, 1961
Age 75

Julian Hampton Parr
Sept. 19, 1877 - Dec. 19, 1935

Our Father
Robert S. Parr
Apr. 18, 1840 - Dec. 12, 1896

Sallie B. Parr
Mar. 25, 1853 - Mar. 7, 1923

Our Grandmother
Emeline H. Carter
Aug. 19, 1820 - Feb. 4, 1900

My Son
H.L. Parr
Nov. 13, 1882 - Oct. 22, 1914

Son
Eugene F. Andrews
1899-1933

Granddaughter
Margaret L. Andrews
1928-1928

Father
James W. Andrews
1859-1914

Mother
Mary R. Andrews
1862-1947

Daughter
Thelma E. Andrews
1906-1925

Granddaughter
Margaret L. Andrews
1928-1928

Aunt
Miranda J. Green
1828-1900

Amanda Griffith
wife of R.R. Puller
Jan. 12, 1872 - Oct. 11, 1898

John K. Cecil
Mar. 14, 1846 - May 31, 1930

Mount Hermon Baptist Church

Olivia Page
wife of John K. Cecil
Mar. 17, 1849 - Aug. 14, 1923

Son
Hewitt R. Barlow
Apr. 26, 1914 - Feb. 16, 1947

Son
Aubrey W. Barlow*
Sept. 5, 1907 - Mar. 25, 1937

Son
Charles L. Barlow
Mar. 21, 1916 - June 8, 1928

Raymond W. Barlow
Virginia Pvt. Air Corps
World War II
Nov. 22, 1919 - Sept. 11, 1944

Father
Bennie A. Barlow
Oct. 9, 1880 - Feb. 27, 1939

Son
Pvt. Raymond W. Barlow
World War II, Va. Air Corps
Nov. 22, 1919 - Sept. 11, 1944
[duplicate]

Beloved Children of
Annie K. & H.W. Pitts
Baby Son
Apr. 25, 1923 - May 3, 1923
Bettie Laverne
Sept. 14, 1935 - May 23, 1936

Harry W. Pitts
1881-1956

Willie Irvin Moore
Virginia S 2 C, U.S.N.R.
World War II
Dec. 28, 1925 - Jul. 12 1947

Wesley E. Samuels
Oct. 14, 1916 - Apr. 23, 1947

*Obituary in The Caroline Progress gives
1934 as death year.

Herbert L. Samuels
Mar. 17, 1914 - Feb. 18, 1936

Harry S. Samuels
Feb. 26, 1927 - Jul. 15, 1950

A. Granville Samuels
Apr. 7, 1919 - June 11, 1960

Reuben Beale Moore, Jr.
Apr. 22, 1938 - May 4, 1952

Our Darling Son
J. Earl Claytor
1916-1935

Our Father
John W. Claytor
May 2, 1887 - Aug. 19, 1956

Clara Mundie

Sallie A. Pitts
July 18, 1886 - July 2, 1951

Ruth Ola
dau. of Mr. & Mrs. J.G. Crisp
Aug. 15, 1912 - June 16, 1913

Robert Pitts
Aug. 25, 1945 - Apr. 14, 1935

Cinderella
wife of Robert Pitts
Oct. 18, 1855 - May 2, 1931

Our Only Daughter
Sabernie C. Pitts
Jan. 17, 1880 - Jul. 22, 1900

Lottie M. Barlow
wife of Harry W. Pitts
Dec. 6, 1886 - Jan. 31, 1908

Rosa B. Martin
wife of Edward D. Barlow
Apr. 8, 1857 - Apr. 15, 1921

Edward D. Barlow
Jan. 5, 1846 - Jan. 12, 1926

Mount Hermon Baptist Church

Carrie F. Barlow
wife of Fornander H. Pitts
Jan. 1, 1873 - Mar. 11, 1896

Eddie Floyd Taylor
Jul. 6, 1915 - Oct. 24, 1948

Eddie Floyd, Jr.
son of Eddie F. and Alice M. Taylor
June 22, 1946 - Sept. 22, 1948

Carl Ball Moore
5 Jul. 1948, age 58

Unmarked Grave

M.B.A.
R.R.
A.S.A.

Lucy A. Allport
Dec. 17, 1842 - Nov. 14, 1924

George W. Allport
April 12, 1850 - Aug. 20, 1891

Mildred P.
wife of John Allport
1808 - Sept. 15, 1888

Our Baby
Charles Marion Allport
Nov. 4, 1883 - Jul. 2, 1884

Father
John William Allport
1872-1958
Mother
Alice Haynes Allport
1881-1954
Mother
Mollie Bell Allport
1877-1907

Audie & Robbie
Infant Children of
Rev. S.U. & S.A. Grimsley

Our Mother
Lelia Page Sirles
wife of W.P. Sirles
Apr. 6, 1852 - Nov. 7, 1899

Father
Woodford P. Sirles
Mar. 15, 1858 - Dec. 12, 1920

Mother
Roberta E. Sirles
Sept. 27, 1870 - Apr. 7, 1914

Ernest Shuman
Born in Darmstadt, Germany
May 7, 1805 - Died Mar. 18, 1902

Joseph A. Shuman
Sept. 20, 1872 - Sept. 7, 1936

Our Darling
Callie Shuman
Oct. 21, 1882 - aged 9 days

Caroline Oteria Shuman
June 1, 1865 - Aug. 30, 1892

Oteria E. Page
wife of C.A. Shuman
Jan. 15, 1842 - June 24, 1890

Charles A. Shuman
Apr. 6, 1835 - Nov. 16, 1918

Thomas W. Green
Co. H, 30 Va. Inf.
C.S.A.

Floyd Green
1900-1901

Florence L. Green
1880-1902

Martha R. Green
1850-1891

Maggie A. Green
1868-1929

Mount Hermon Baptist Church

Stone Without Inscription

Annie Wayne Kelley
Jul. 30, 1895 - Jan. 29, 1897

KELLY
William Henry
1861-1942
Clara Green
1876-1950

Our Father and Mother
Addison Louis Houston
Jul. 17, 1811 - Jul. 31, 1892
Martha Ellen Houston
Jan. 18, 1819 - Aug. 31, 1892

John F. Covington
Co. K, 47 Va. Inf.
C.S.A.

Mt. Horeb Church, which is located 12 miles southeast of Bowling Green at Lorne, Virginia, was organized in 1773 as Reed's Church. The first minister was imprisoned for 6 months for preaching without a license. Samuel Davies, of nearby Hanover County, was the founder of Princeton University and of the Presbyterian Church in America. He occasionally spoke at Reed's Church, and introduced Presbyterianism to the County.

In 1840, a new brick meeting house was built on the original site. Both Concord Baptist and Mount Hermon Baptist churches were formed from Mt. Horeb. Another meeting house was erected on a different site on an acre tract donated to the church in 1853 by J.R. Mason. At that time the name was changed from Reed's Church to Mt. Horeb. The structure presently used is the fourth building for this congregation, and was dedicated on December 23, 1890.

This site was visited on September 23, 1961.

Frances A. Baughan
1834-1897
Age 63 yrs.

Richard J. Baughan
1813-1893
Age 71 yrs.

Grace W. Barlow
Jan. 23, 1895 - Oct. 22, 1918

Sallie Williams
Aug. 23, 1877 - Jan. 14, 1906

H.H. Dyson
Aug. 1, 1841 - Feb. 10, 1915

Annie W. Dyson
Jun. 2, 1860 - Jan. 23, 1925

Annie Lee
wife of Lucas W. Dyson
Mar. 11, 1893 - Oct. 24, 1918

Mrs. Fannie Edwards
Jul. 4, 1933
My Husband
Henry C. Edwards
Apr. 10, 1846 - Feb. 15, 1925

Welford Dyson
Apr. 23, 1906 - May 3, 1940

Kermit W.
son of E.S. & S.C. Barlow
1930-1934

Wilbert J. Blanton
Oct. 20, 1877 - Sept. 12, 1936

Frank Ernest Shuman
Aug. 12, 1849 - Dec. 12, 1935

Nannie West Shuman
Jan. 5, 1860 - Nov. 26, 1935

Mt. Vernon Methodist Church

Located off Route 2, 5½ miles northeast on Route 600, at Lorne, Virginia. This church was first organized in the early 1800's at Vernon Farm, the home of Mrs. James Thomas, Sr. The present building was erected in 1852 and constructed of brick fired in a kiln on the premises. The church was originally known as Vernon Methodist Church, then Mt. Vernon Methodist Episcopal Church South, and finally Mt. Vernon Methodist Church. An addition was made to the building in 1986.

This site was visited on September 23, 1961.

Infant son of
A.C. & Pearl A. Carneal
Feb. 6, 1926

Lemuel Adams
1873-1918

Sallie D. Adams
1875-1958

Willie R. Samuels
July 2, 1872 - Apr. 1, 1956

Our Son
Earnest R. Baldwin
Feb. 12, 1936 - Jan. 31, 1938

Unmarked Grave

Thomas J. Harrison
Feb. 6, 1833 - Aug. 3, 1903

N.W. Pollard
Nov. 9, 1890 - Jan. 15, 1932

Barton Russell Dyson
Died Dec. 24, 1948
Age 36 yrs.

Mrs. Nannie Southworth
Died 1956

Roland L. Carneal
Mar. 10, 1868 - Jan. 20, 1943

Mollie B. Carneal
Nov. 20, 1868 - May 11, 1954

Loretta E. Southworth
Oct. 18, 1911 - Feb. 18, 1913

Floy E. Southworth
Jul. 19, 1913 - Feb. 12, 1914

M. Louise Southworth
Feb. 25, 1918 - Dec. 25, 1918

J.P. Shepherdson
May 4, 1844 - May 17, 1918

Emma C. Shepherdson
Oct. 12, 1853 - Jan. 12, 1926

Richard P. Ancarrow
Aug. 21, 1857 - Jan. 9, 1934

John William Ancarrow
Dec. 24, 1850 - Feb. 9, 1925

Mary Bassford
Feb. 22, 1853 - Feb. 11, 1925

Dorris Ancarrow Williams
Apr. 7, 1911 - Jul. 27, 1916

Robert Allen Thomas
Oct. 25, 1888 - Aug. 11, 1927

James H. Thomas
Apr. 1, 1853 - Jan. 19, 1918

Mt. Vernon Methodist Church

Mary Anne Thomas
Oct. 21, 1895 - Jul. 4, 1897
Lucy Alice Thomas
Mar. 11, 1847 - Jan. 24, 1923

Marion Thomas Carlton
Died Oct. 19, 1954
Age 67 yrs.

Charlie W. Seymour
1881-1944

Lucy T. Fox
Apr. 29, 1895 - Dec. 31, 1937

Woodrow Wilson Pate
1944-1955

Jordan M. Southworth
Virginia
Corp. 318 Inf. 80 Div.
Aug. 8, 1934

John G. Dillard
Oct. 29, 1878 - Oct. 12, 1945

Bernice Gray Martola
Aug. 29, 1916 - Aug. 23, 1950

Samuel P. Thomas
Dec. 16, 1839 - Dec. 27, 1920

Samuel E. Dillard
Jul. 20, 1899 - Jan. 26, 1919

Charles Edward Dillard
Sept. 17, 1852 - Apr. 29, 1910

Etta L. Dillard
Nov. 2, 1869 - Jun. 8, 1928

Woodford B. Dillard
Nov. 13, 1895 - Jul. 17, 1926

C.B. Southworth
Jun. 4, 1852 - Feb. 24, 1926

Julian A. Williams
Virginia
Pvt. 755 Railway Shop Bn.
World War II
Apr. 13, 1898 - Jan. 21, 1949

Annie Smith Williams
1858-1927

Clarence Williams
Died Jan. 23, 1961
Age 81 yrs.

James Wesley Embrey
Died Mar. 10, 1918
[unmarked]

Woody Gray
Nov. 14, 1891 - Nov. 14, 1891

Charles Clarence Thomas
Oct. 2, 1905 - Sept. 4, 1920

Janie Dyson Thomas
May 30, 1879 - Nov. 23, 1937

Charles Vaden Thomas
May 26, 1872 - Feb. 20, 1948

William Clayton Crow
Jan. 25, 1927 - Feb. 18, 1928

Mildred Catherine Crowe
[illegible]

Lillian Mae Samuels
Died Jul. 17, 1956
Age 14 yrs.

Mrs. C.L. Samuel
Dec. 21, 1888 - Jul. 24, 1932

Baby Samuel
Jul. 21, 1932 - Jul. 22, 1932

Grace Samuel
Mar. 5, 1929 - Mar. 22, 1929

Charlie J. Southworth
Mar. 11, 1879 - Apr. 2, 1960

Mt. Vernon Methodist Church

Allie Walter Adams
Nov. 15, 1875 - Aug. 24, 1943

William Reece
Jul. 20, 1937 - Jul. 30, 1937

William Reece
Sept. 9, 1868 - Jul. 21, 1939

Lola M. Reece
Jul. 4, 1875 - Sept. 4, 1939

Allen Reece
Jun. 7, 1914 - Jan. 14, 1952

Roseboro Reece
Sept. 9, 1908 - Jun. 27, 1930

Ella Reece
Aug. 20, 1909 - Apr. 30, 1929

Emma A. Garnett
1865-1930

John W. Garnett
1853-1935

Birtie B. Atkins Garnett
June 1895 - Apr. 1937

Mrs. M.A. Loving
Jun. 19, 1893 - Feb. 15, 1928

Mrs. Melvina J. Hale
wife of J.S. Hale
Born Mar. 13, 1857 - Died Jul. 1, 1929

Mrs. N.E. Bullock
Feb. 27, 1892 - Apr. 25, 1926

Sidney M. Bullock
Dec. 22, 1922 - Jan. 21, 1923

John S. Hale
Apr. 29, 1860 - May 17, 1939

John Hale Street
Jan. 26, 1922 - Oct. 25, 1926

Infant daughter of Tate & Lucy Bullock
Jan. 30, 1932 - Jan. 30, 1932

Charlie F. Street, Sr.
Apr. 17, 1885 - Jan. 7, 1949

Pearl Hale Street
Apr. 25, 1886 -

P. Maurice Barlow
Mar. 10, 1869 - Feb. 15, 1941

Audrey B. Barlow
Jan. 31, 1893 - Feb. 14, 1938

Willie L. Chenault
Aug. 19, 1866 - Feb. 22, 1941

Mary F. Chenault
Jun. 15, 1870 - Oct. 1, 1941

Ella W. Atkins
May 8, 1862 - Dec. 25, 1933

James D. Atkins
Jul. 14, 1856 - Mar. 7, 1914

Many Unmarked Graves

Site of Port Royal Methodist Church

This church, which was located on Lot 49 in Port Royal, Virginia, was used at various times by Episcopal, Presbyterian, Methodist, and Baptist congregations. As early as 1819, it was used as an Episcopal church where Rev. Joseph R. Andrus, of nearby St. Paul's Church in King George County, conducted services. By 1844, it was known as the Methodist Church South, where members met until 1927 when it was purchased by the Baptist Church. After membership reached over 80, enrollment declined in the 1940's, and by 1944, services had stopped.

The last building, constructed of wood, was built around 1900, after the original was destroyed by a cyclone in 1870.

For nearly 30 years this church building stood unoccupied. Meanwhile the Baptists from this area built Memorial Baptist Church on Lot 13 of Port Royal, where cornerstone ceremonies were held in April 1952. Many of the former members of Port Royal Baptist Church joined the new church.

By the time this site was visited on December 2, 1961, most of the structure's window panes were broken out, and birds had nested inside. The carpeting was still in place, and the altar furniture was strewn about. The interior was not plastered but had beaded ceiling boards on the side walls. There were some small black books in shelving to the left of the altar. The grounds were littered, and the rear of the property was overgrown by brush and trees. The cemetery on both sides of the building showed signs of some maintenance--the right side having been sodded for the winter. Since that visit the church was torn down in March 1977, and the cemetery now occupies the entire site and is maintained.

Ralph Fall, in his book Hidden Valley, on page 236 therein, lists the following persons buried here in unmarked graves: William Hicks (great uncle of Robert A. Hicks), Henry or Benjamin Hicks (brother of Robert A. Hicks), Pinckney Gibbs Ennis (grandmother of Robert A. Hicks), Sonny Burruss, and Lee Rice. Also buried here are many members of the Roach family.

Clarence F. Hicks Jan. 16, 1868 - Feb. 29, 1932	Jan. 6, 1828 - Nov. 1, 1891
Mary Ennis Hicks Jul. 28, 1867 - Nov. 15, 1945	George W. Edwards 1845-1923
Chas. Preston Roach Sept. 20, 1856 - Feb. 25, 1947	Ella V. Edwards 1849-1916
Sarah J. Owens Feb. 6, 1852 - May 3, 1942	Robert C. Watts Oct. 28, 1881 - Dec. 4, 1929
Our Mother Mary F. Owens	Mabel Estelle Watts Apr. 27, 1889 - Apr. 26, 1954

Site of Port Royal Methodist Church

Ryland S. Watts
1892-1942

My Husband
Charles H. Watts
Jan. 21, 1889 - Jul. 22, 1937

Jack P. Watts
June 2, 1895 - Jul. 21, 1948

Our Father
Daniel L. Rollins
Nov. 27, 1871 - Oct. 25, 1940

Mother
Ida B. Rollins
Oct. 22, 1877 - June 28, 1948

My Husband
Cecil M. Brown
Sept. 21, 1896 - Jan. 27, 1942

Father
Horace L. Steelman
1844-1909

Providence Baptist Church

Providence Baptist Church is located 6 miles southeast of Bowling Green, Virginia, and on the west side of Route 14. The cemetery is off the road which runs between DeJarnette Post Office and File Post Office, and reached by turning at St. James Church and going nearly .2 miles into the woods.

The church, erected in 1837, originally faced north, but the structure was later altered so that it faced the road. The structure had a flat shingled roof, a gallery ran the full length of the back and side, and the seats were elevated to accommodate viewing of the minister who stood in a box pulpit. It had two doors, a large one on the front in which the white people entered, and a side door which was used by black members. James F. Covington wrote the deed for the cemetery land which was taken from the Green family estate, and given by Mr. Green to the church trustees. The area consists of two acres.

Though once a prosperous church, by the 1970's the congregation had dwindled to a dozen or so attending members. In 1876, the church closed its doors, placed its records in the Baptist Historical Society, and sold the property to a black congregation.

Evidence of many unmarked graves is found from mounds and sinks. Among those buried there in unmarked graves are Mrs. Effie Pitts Crowell, Raymond Martin (5-year old son of Mr. and Mrs. Jesse Martin, who died January 23, 1920), Jesse Martin (who was buried here February 6, 1921), Coleman Houston, Miss Molly Houston, the first wife of Jack Beasley, Jesse Martin (who was buried February 6, 1921), and Henry C. Beazley, father of Mrs. C.D. Andrews, who died in December 1922, aged 72.

This site was visited April 27, 1963.

Georgia C. Brooks
November 20, 1853 - June 8, 1954

Festus Brooks
1842-1920

Ruby Pleasant Brooks
April 7, 1907 - June 22, 1909

Thomas Festus Brooks
March 5, 1926

Bettie G. Poates
March 15, 1883 - January 1, 1953

Bettie C. Poates
September 15, 1855-November 15, 1931

L.F. Poates
July 28, 1853 - April 18, 1917

J.L. Poates
September 15, 1893-December 28, 1915

R.J. Beasley
December 31, 1865 - March 18, 1932

Cora Lee Beasley
November 1, 1961, age 86 years

Lucile Whittaker
February 1, 1921 - January 5, 1925

Providence Baptist Church

Everett Bradley
son of Thomas W. & Edmonia Barlow
Beasley
November 6, 1892 - June 2, 1910

Edmonia L. Barlow Beasley
April 19, 1851 - March 25, 1939

Thomas Wilson Beasley
January 25, 1862 - December 29, 1961

Sallie J. Pugh
June 9, 1893 - Age 32 years
Erected by her Mother
Mrs. S.J. Carneal

Sarah J. Carneal
Age 79 years

Located .5 mile from Chilesburg, Virginia, and 3 miles from the North Anna River, on Route 738. This congregation was organized in 1841. The present building was originally County Line Baptist Church, but was sold to the Methodist congregation in 1841, when County Line was moved further up the road to the site now occupied by the County Line Baptist Church cemetery.

This site was visited in 1961.

Father
Leonard Phillippe
1894-1954

Baby daughter of
Clyde and Hattie Morefield
June 10, 1934

Isaac D. Phillippe
Mar. 7, 1885 - Aug. 14, 1949
[Father]
Louise J. Phillippe
Jul. 31, 1885 - May 11, 1960
[Mother]

Andrew J. Phillippe
1865-1950
Sophia C. Phillippe
1862-1928

Julia A. Thompson
Jun. 7, 1850 - Jun. 8, 1940
James L. Thompson
Dec. 17, 1850 - Dec. 24, 1935

Margaret Carrie
daughter of James & Julia Thompson
Aug. 18, 1882 - Feb. 9, 1925

Charles Hiram Thompson
Feb. 28, 1887 - Jun. 21, 1960

Henry W. Hart
Oct. 6, 1887 - Mar. 9, 1955
Noble W. Hart
June 2, 1892 -

Bessie Shoupe
Jan. 24, 1892 - Mar. 2, 1937

Stephen Blaine Shupe
May 11, 1890 - Jun. 5, 1929

Mother
Bessie E. Rankin
1894-1934

Mother
Ellen Duvall
Jul. 30, 1860 - Feb. 28, 1948

Father
E.M. Duvall
Dec. 26, 1860 - June 26, 1941

Annie R. Garland
Mar. 1, 1873 - Jun. 13, 1955
Edward J. Garland
Nov. 10, 1864 - Feb. 21, 1933

Iva G. Scott
1896-
Lacy C. Scott
1897-1950

Son
Bernard M. Durrett
1935-1946

John Henry Morefield
Sept. 19, 1875 - Jul. 6, 1956
His wife
Mary Emma Fritts
Apr. 6, 1876 - May 5, 1939

124

Rehoboth Methodist Church

Wilbur D. Colaw
1857-1943
Nora B. Colaw
1872-1944

Lizzie D. Peyton
Mar. 7, 1872 - Jan. 4, 1938
John A. Peyton
Apr. 2, 1876 -

James Rosser Peyton
Aug. 9, 1878 - Jul. 8, 1958
[Father]
Mary Burruss Peyton
Nov. 13, 1882 - Aug. 19, 1921
[Mother]

J. Edward Burruss
1859-1931
[Father]
Lena S. Burruss
1861-1952
[Mother]

Sophia Waller Hancock
Jul. 17, 1875 - Jul. 12, 1952

John Wesley Hancock
Feb. 8, 1865 - Jan. 17, 1918

Infant son of
John and Alice Hancock Moss
Aug. 29, 1938

Kate Partlow
May 5, 1857 - Jan. 23, 1944
[Mother]
J. Lancelot Partlow
Jan. 21, 1859 - Sept. 1, 1919
[Father]

Willie E. Partlow
Feb. 8, 1892 - Nov. 28, 1956
[Husband]
Maggie N. Partlow
Jan. 24, 1892 -

Grave With Cement Marker

George A. Rotzler
Jan. 1, 1881 - Nov. 3, 1951

George G. Blanton
1861-1933
Nannie M. Blanton
1859-1930

Two Unmarked Graves

Arden Johnson Eastridge
Jun. 12, 1939 - Jan. 23, 1959

Joyce Angelia Eastridge
Feb. 25, 1941 - Mar. 28, 1941

Jean M. Greene
1910-
Alpha E. Greene, Jr.
1912-1954
[Mason]

James R. Greene
1848-1936
[Father]
Ellen T. Green
1862-1949

Charlie Ulice Leathers
May 24, 1878 - Apr. 27, 1957

W.E. Leathers
Jul. 28, 1851 - Jun. 27, 1926

Mary E. Leathers
Mar. 10, 1854 - Mar. 30, 1925

John W. Southworth
Aug. 18, 1875 - Jul. 18, 1952

Mildred D. Southworth
Jul. 14, 1871 - Jan. 16, 1934

Two Unmarked Graves

Ida Peyton Walsh
May 22, 1872 - Feb. 19, 1950

Arris T. Walsh
Aug. 21, 1867 - Apr. 25, 1934

125

Rehoboth Methodist Church

Martha Ann Peyton
Dec. 24, 1848 - Apr. 5, 1926

James M. Peyton
Apr. 4, 1841 - Apr. 16, 1935

Mabel Lavaughn Sacra
Feb. 16, 1924 - May 19, 1943

James Donald Sacra
Oct. 6, 1938 - Oct. 18, 1938

Mother
Laura Rankin Watson
Nov. 13, 1868 - May 29, 1951

Stanley Thomas Rankin
Mar. 17, 1894 - Aug. 18, 1938

Located north of Bowling Green, Virginia, just off Route 2 at Corbin Post Office. Established about 1840, the present building of Round Oak Baptist Church was erected in 1852, with additions being made in the 20th century.

In August 1840, fifteen members of Liberty Baptist Church were dismissed by letter for the purpose of organizing a church in the Corbin area. On Saturday, October 10, 1840, eleven of these members met for the purpose of organizing Round Oak Baptist Church. Lawrence Battaille was chosen pastor and he served from 1840 until 1847. In 1840, an addition was made to the building, due to the growing congregation. The second addition was made in 1915, and another in 1950. The education building was added in the 1960's, and memorial windows were given by members of the church.

There are 141 Confederate soldiers buried in the church cemetery. Each grave has a marker, but none bear inscriptions.

This site was visited December 2, 1961.

Silas J. Sale
June 25, 1876 - Oct. 26, 1948

Etta Ryerson Sale
Jan. 23, 1876 - Aug. 23, 1947

Clairette L. Sale
Aug. 31, 1911 - Mar. 3, 1923

Anthony J. Sale
May 6, 1843 - Jan. 16, 1918

Emma Ella Sale
devoted wife of A.J. Sale
Dec. 23, 1853 - July 16, 1915

S. Coleman Thomas
Mar. 30, 1884 - Sept. 10, 1939

William P. Flippo
Sept. 1849 - Jan. 1916
His wife
Almira Y. Flippo
Sept. 1857 - Jan. 1921

Irene Flippo Sale
wife of T.B. Sale, Sr.
Feb. 6, 1889 - Sept. 22, 1953

Benjamin W. Flippo
1852-1928

Belva
Beloved wife of J.B. Flippo
Aged 35 years

James B. Flippo
1886-1951

Pattie Smith
wife of J.B. Flippo
1893-1949

Joseph Mills
Sept. 13, 1890 - Sept. 17, 1919
[Woodmen of the World]

Private Ernest C. Purks
H Co. 38th Infantry
Nov. 25, 1888 - Oct. 8, 1918
Killed in Battle in France

127

Round Oak Baptist Church

John H. Skinner
Oct. 20, 1871 - Aug. 29, 1932

Georgie E. Skinner
Jan. 11, 1876 - May 7, 1937

Gladys White Skinner
Mar. 29, 1901 - Sept. 29, 1950

Leonard Franklin Skinner
April 1, 1899 -

Francis Wilson Denson
Feb. 17, 1861 - Dec. 19, 1940

Maria Brokaw
Feb. 16, 1862 - Mar. 9, 1940

William B. Hayden
Apr. 11, 1891 - Dec. 22, 1922

Henrietta P. Hayden
May 17, 1888 - Mar. 15, 1937

Homer C. Hayden
May 29, 1894 - Mar. 4, 1957

Oscar V. Mills
Jul. 8, 1895 - Mar. 23, 1923

Mary G. Mills
Mar. 25, 1888 - Aug. 15, 1959

Wm. M. Hayden
May 23, 1859 - Jul. 6, 1937

Georgie F. Hayden
Dec. 28, 1859 - Mar. 4, 1952

Robert A. Hayden
Sept. 12, 1897 - Sept. 10, 1919

Father
Marion N. Thomas
June 6, 1880 - Feb. 2, 1919

Mother
Maggie S. Thomas
Jan. 4, 1880 - Apr. 29, 1919

Mother
Isabelle Sale Elliott
Nov. 19, 1891 - Oct. 6, 1922

Brother
Lowery N. Thomas
May 29, 1906 - Jul. 17, 1925

Peter P. Brokaw
Mar. 5, 1836 - Nov. 17, 1927

Margaret C. Brokaw
Feb. 12, 1830 - May 26, 1917

Henry G. Brokaw
Sept. 16, 1867 - Feb. 7, 1937

Mary C. Tompkins
1864-1951

Nannie D. Flippo
1854-1924

Ellen D. Dillard
Died June 18, 1924

G.C. Surles
Dec. 11, 1885 - Oct. 20, 1922

Luther M. Surles
Sept. 16, 1920 - Dec. 16, 1922

Father
Bennie H. Mills
June 19, 1886 - Sept. 11, 1933

Mother
Ollie C. Mills
Dec. 2, 1892 - Jul. 28, 1925

Reginald W. James
Apr. 8, 1922 - Apr. 19, 1923

Harold Mills
Apr. 3, 1903 - Oct. 29, 1932

John Wilson Rhoday
Apr. 27, 1914 - Aug. 28, 1922

128

Round Oak Baptist Church

John W. Rhody
Jan. 30, 1885 - Dec. 26, 1952

Harriet P. Rhody
Apr. 10, 1885 -

Joseph F. Jones
1876-1931

Father-Mother
Josiah S. Thomas
Aug. 3, 1857 - June 5, 1959
Martha E. Thomas
Jan. 12, 1860 - Nov. 4, 1943

Mother
Florence G. Marshall
Sept. 4, 1902 - July 14, 1943

Frank P. Farmer
Aug. 8, 1876 - Sept. 21, 1945

Hattie L. Farmer
Dec. 7, 1884 -

Marjorie L. Jones
Sept. 13, 1920 - Aug. 7, 1923

Walter W. Purks
1851-1925

Lucy E. Purks
Nov. 25, 1856 - Feb. 27, 1936

Farley B. Drish
Oct. 7, 1898 - May 31, 1929

Churchill Brown
Sept. 4, 1860 - Aug. 25, 1927

Maggie S. Brown
May 14, 1866 - Mar. 16, 1941

Lewis G. Jones
Oct. 6, 1863 - Nov. 27, 1944

Bettie G. Purks
Sept. 17, 1867 - Dec. 17, 1927

William B. Jones
Aug. 10, 1866 - Sept. 4, 1949

Frederick W. Oesterheld
Father
Dec. 3, 1875 - Sept. 9, 1957

Alice Skinner Oesterheld
Mother
June 7, 1885 - Jan. 19, 1930

Ralph Conway Barlow
Sept. 8, 1939 - Sept. 25, 1939

James Madkson Dillard
Jan. 18, 1877 - Oct. 1, 1937

Kate Pugh Thomas
Sept. 2, 1881 - Jul. 15, 1960

Ivy Louise Thomas
June 7, 1912 - Feb. 24, 1932

Elic Thomas
May 13, 1904 - Apr. 4, 1952

Strauther Jones
Feb. 12, 1872 - Feb. 4, 1930

Wayne Lee Sale
Dec. 8, 1944 - Mar. 11, 1954

Clyde G. Sale
May 6, 1933 - Apr. 10, 1936

Ottis L. Sale
May 17, 1932 - Lived 7 hrs.
Two buds of love, now with God above.

George W. Adle
Mar. 28, 1855 - Jul. 28, 1930

Sirlinia H. Sale
Sept. 17, 1859 - Jan. 23, 1941

Clarence B. Sale
Mar. 20, 1891 - Dec. 4, 1950

Round Oak Baptist Church

Husband
Henry O. Denson
1897-1936

Warner Bruce Brown
Virginia P.F.C., Co. A
318 Infantry, W.W. I
Nov. 23, 1893 - Mar. 5, 1960

Josephine T. Brown
Jan. 2, 1897 -

William W. Mills, Jr.
Virginia, Pvt. U.S. Army
June 17, 1903 - Nov. 16, 1933

J. Samuel Purks
Died Feb. 22, 1933

Fannie E. Purks
Died Dec. 28, 1931

Allice Elwood M. Goings
Nov. 23, 1876 - June 12, 1931

Susie Jones Goings
Aug. 6, 1882 - Mar. 28, 1950

Lillian A. Jones
Jan. 22, 1906 - Nov. 4, 1931

Alvin W. Jones
Mar. 9, 1900 - May 4, 1947

Walter F. Self
Apr. 9, 1865 - Oct. 13, 1918
His wife
Addie V. Sale
Mar. 3, 1866 - Mar. 26, 1932

William J. Self
Apr. 28, 1895 - Oct. 29, 1942

Henry Arthur Brown
Died Nov. 4, 1960
Aged 63 yrs. 7 mos. 7 days

Taft B. Mills
Died Mar. 13, 1958
Aged 44 yrs. [ ] mos. 21 days

Littleberry A. Mills
Oct. 4, 1872 - Aug. 24, 1938

Lester L. Green
Oct. 15, 1879 - Apr. 23, 1933

Mattie A. Green
Feb. 20, 1881 - Jul. 1, 1956

Dellie B. Klock
Nov. 16, 1873 - Nov. 20, 1939

Frances Sale Klock
Dec. 4, 1876 - Nov. 27, 1952

James Cornelius Peters
Died May 26, 1961
Age 63

Lucy Alma Dillard
1840-1905

James Madison Dillard
1823-1895

Calvin Martin
Thornton's Co., Virginia L. Arty.
C.S.A.

Samuel Perks
Confederate Soldier

Samuel Purks
1835-1926
Sarah Purks
1837-1901
Their Children
Sam - George - Nannie
Ella E. Purks
1870-1948
Fannie A. Purks
1873-19__

Mosley M. Mullen
Co. A - 40 Virginia Infantry
C.S.A.

Lannie Howard
Died Nov. 15, 1918
Aged 34 years

130

Round Oak Baptist Church

Horace E. Cox
1852-1931

Father
William B. Jones
Sept. 22, 1837 - Aug. 31, 1908

Mother
S. Jane Proctor Jones
Feb. 28, 1854 - Mar. 7, 1906

James R. Fountaine
Oct. 11, 1864 - May 31, 1931

Father J.B. Greene
1845-1907

James Shelton
1868-1926
His wife
Fannie E. Purks
1865-1924
[Woodmen of the World]

Bettie L.
wife of William Dodd
Aug. 12, 1869 - Jan. 30, 1891

James A. Cash
Oct. 10, 1855 - Jan. 22, 1954

Fannie Brown Cash
Wife of James A.
Sept. 18, 1858
Feb. 13, 1936

E.B. Jones
1868-1941

Annie H. Jones
1883-1959

Richard Wellington Alvis
Died Apr. 15, 1961
Aged 82 yrs. 8 mos. 25 days

Lizzie Cash Alvis
May 21, 1878 - June 24, 1920

J.T. Carter
Nov. 5, 1840 - June 17, 1903

Bettie Carter
July 4, 1852 - June 15, 1917

Marion E. Carter
Jan. 10, 1910 - Nov. 19, 1918

David D. McWhirt
Jan. 18, 1906 - May 2, 1952

Mary P. McWhirt
Apr. 9, 1907 -

John G. Samuel
Died Mar. 29, 1911

John H. Samuel
Died May 19, 1916

Conway G. Carter
Apr. 22, 1912 - Oct. 27, 1944

Andrew W. Brown
Apr. 26, 1871 - Mar. 19, 1943

Carrie V. Brown
Aug. 19, 1871 - Nov. 6, 1934

John T. Carter
Jan. 28, 1907 - Feb. 12, 1908

Garland C. Sale
Nov. 6, 1918 - Feb. 3, 1941

Walter A. Sale
Oct. 6, 1880 - Nov. 25, 1950

H.S. Purks
1876-1937

Chrissie A. Chilton
June 15, 1901 -

Linda J. Chilton
Oct. 14, 1903 - May 24, 1955

131

Round Oak Baptist Church

Mother
Elizabeth Purks
Oct. 8, 1872 - July 6, 1938

Father
Thos. L. Jenkins
Nov. 11, 1877 - Sept. 6, 1906

James M. Skinner
Feb. 22, 1871 - Mar. 4, 1952

Willie Ann Kennedy
Aug. 10, 1877 - Apr. 28, 1951

Stephen T. Kennedy
Sept. 5, 1866 - Feb. 6, 1920

Melisia, wife of R.F. Dillard
Nov. 27, 1821 - June 7, 1897

Sgt. Robert F. Dillard
Thornton's Co., Virginia Light Arty.
C.S.A.

Wesley C. Purks
Nov. 7, 1846 - Apr. 10, 1932

Laura O. Purks
Mar. 14, 1867 - Aug. 23, 1944

Benjamin F. Grimes
1876-1947

Phebe T. Grimes
1869-

Father
Roy C. Purks
Jan. 6, 1872 - July 15, 1945

Thomas Purks
Oct. 25, 1865 - Mar. 5, 1948

Willie M. Lumpkin
Dec. 2, 1874 - Feb. 13, 1920

Lucian M. Lumpkin
June 16, 1872 - Aug. 6, 1945

Florence L. Lumpkin
Aug. 20, 1886 - Mar. 4, 1951

Sidney Emmitt
Died Aug. 17, 1961
Aged 76 yrs.

[141 Graves With Small Uninscribed
Stones]

132

Sts. Cyril and Metlodious Catholic Church

Located 1.4 miles west of Lebanon Church, on Route 605, near Welch, Virginia. This congregation divided from nearby St. Mary's Catholic Church, and built the present chapel which was consecrated on July 6, 1924. The church later closed and the membership returned to St. Mary's, using this building as a community hall for St. Mary's.

Mary M. Stanik
Died Jul. 9, 1954
Age 81 yrs.

Mary Parisek
Aug. 15, 1881 - Mar. 28, 1955

Paul P. Parisek
Jun. 29, 1881 - Oct. 30, 1952

John Michel Newchok
Died Sept. 5, 1961
Age 55 yrs.

Three Unmarked Graves

Grave With Wooden Cross

Helen Molnar
Jun. 15, 1888 - Jun. 17, 1948

Grave With Wooden Cross

Hermina Simulcik
Na Rodena 1868
Zomrela 1919

John Simulcik
Died Dec. 21, 1957
Age 87 yrs.

Tu Spociva
Viktor Simulcik
Ro Deni Feb. 9, 1912
Zomrel Nov. 21, 1931

Tu Spociva
Jan Simulcik, Jr.
Ro Deni Dec. 27, 1895
Zomrel Dec. 10, 1935

Joseph Majerak, Sr.
Born May 7, 1891, Czechoslovakia
Died Aug. 5, 1958, Richmond Memorial
Hospital, Richmond, Va.
Buried Welche's Cemetery, Caroline
County, Va.

Father
John Chudacek
1888-1943

Mother
Caroline Chudacek
1896-1936

Mary Aversa
Sept. 10, 1905 - Oct. 20, 1950

John J. Michaliga
Apr. 15, 1883 - Aug. 9, 1950

Theresa Michaliga
Oct. 17, 1888 - Feb. 13, 1958

Albina M. Gaby
Dec. 16, 1909 - Jul. 31, 1942

John Gaby, Sr.
Apr. 27, 1870 - Aug. 30, 1952

Otec
Ozef Sitarik
1877-1911

Sts. Cyril & Metlodious Catholic Church

William Newchock
Born Nov. 18, 1915
Died July 19, 1942

Tu Spociva
Jozef Vnucak
Narodeny 1881
Zomrel 20 Jan. 1921

Tu Spociva
Stefan Parisek
Rodeni Vo Brezh 1884
Zomrel Dec. 9, 1936

Tu Spociva
Anna Apalka
Rod. Jun. 18, 1907
Zom. Jun. 18, 1911

Steve C. Glembo, Jr.
Jun. 29, 1910 - Mar. 28, 1957

Steve Glembo
Jun. 24, 1876 - Nov. 22, 1946

St. Margaret's Episcopal Church

Located at Ruther Glen, Virginia. St. Margaret's Parish, established in 1720, was one of the three original parishes of Caroline County and encompassed the area lying between the Mattapony and the North Anna-Pamunkey boundaries. In the beginning, St. Margaret's Parish extended beyond Caroline into King William and Spotsylvania counties, but in 1742 the General Assembly placed the lands outside Caroline County in other parishes. Since that time all of St. Margaret's Parish has been in Caroline County.

There were three large brick churches in this parish: Chesterfield, Bull Church and Reedy Church. When the old churches were destroyed, an unpretentious frame clapboard building was erected near Ruther Glen to take their place. In 1866, the members of the Episcopal Church in Bowling Green transferred their membership to this church.

This site was visited December 26, 1961.

Frances Adelia Wood
May 23, 1849 - May 1, 1926

James Edwin Smith
Aug. 15, 1840 - Mar. 9, 1919
His wife
Wilhemina Wood
Feb. 5, 1852 - Feb. 18, 1908

Florence C. Hunter
Nov. 1, 1890 - Oct. 13, 1953

Jas. Hunter, Jr.
Nov. 16, 1843 - Dec. 11, 1906

Florence Coleman
wife of Jas. Hunter, Jr.
Mar. 21, 1857 - Mar. 6, 1929

Unmarked Grave

Warren B. Smith
Sept. 15, 1882 - Jan. 24, 1949

Our darling
William James
son of M.E. & E.S. Quarles
Feb. 9, 1907 - Apr. 1, 1911

St. Mary's Catholic Church

The cemetery is located from the church on Route 626, near Woodford, Virginia. The Roman Catholic Church had its beginning in Caroline County in 1908 when a number of Slovaks came to the County from New Jersey and Pennsylvania. They settled around the villages of Woodford, Milford and Guinea. Their first house of worship was old Todd's Tavern, also known as Villesboro, at the intersection of U.S. Route 2 and the Woodford Road. This was eventually replaced in 1913 by a chapel near Woodford which they named St. Mary's.

By 1918, the Roman Catholic congregation at St. Mary's had prospered to the point that they had their visions on a second chapel. This was built at nearby Welch, Virginia, and was named Sts. Cyril and Metlodious Catholic Church.

Marvin T. Beazley
Died Oct. 12, 1958
Age 56 yrs.

Peter Yurik
Jun. 29, 1881 - Aug. 21, 1959

Mary Anna Yurik
Apr. 23, 1884 - Sept. 12, 1958

John M. Maholick
1876-1960

Ella Maholick
1880-1954

Agnes Ondrusek
1866-1937

Teofil Ondrusek
1864-1943

John Kelly Wickouski
Died Jun. 19, 1961
Age 51 yrs.

Albert L. Wickouski
1911-1942

Albert Randolph
son of John Wickouski
Mar. 6, 1944 - Mar. 8, 1944

Nelliek Wickouski
1885-1957

Joseph Wickouski
1875-1937

Francis Wickouski
1904-1919

John Maslanko
Mar. 16, 1878 - Mar. 6, 1957

Mary E. Maslanko
Aug. 13, 1877 - Jun. 8, 1959

John Z. Koday
Feb. 21, 1879 - Jun. 2, 1947

Zofie A. Koday
May 14, 1884 - Oct. 11, 1955

Stephen Zak
1892-1946

Joseph J. Latka
Mar. 17, 1891 - Sept. 3, 1942

Joseph J. Stefaniga
1882-1942

Veronica S. Stefaniga
1886-

St. Mary's Catholic Church

Steve A. Treblic
Jan. 30, 1865 - Nov. 8, 1954

Mary M. Treblic
Jul. 13, 1880 - Feb. 10, 1956

Survey Showing Location of Reedy Church, 1820

St. Paul's United Methodist Church

This church is located in the forks of State Route 654 and 656 on Burruss's Mill Road, beyond an old oak tree which has guarded its site for about 250 years. The church is built at the site of the former Reedy Church, for which the Reedy Church Magistral District of the County derives its name.

Francis Scott bought the Reedy Church property at public auction. The first church used by the Methodist congregation here was a log building that had a dirt floor. In 1852, Francis Scott donated the site to the congregation, and a structure of brick was built for the St. Paul's Methodist Church South.

The first Woman's Foreign Missionary Society ever organized in Methodism was here at St. Paul's Church. Because the original brick had deteriorated, another layer of brick, as a veneer, was added to the structure in 1966. At the same time a portico was added to the sanctuary, and an educational building was added to the facility.

This site was visited September 23, 1961.

Benjamin V. Claytor
Oct. 8, 1888 - May 19, 1953

Mary F. Long
1848-1921

Margaret A. Claytor
1855-1924

Charles L. Claytor
Jul. 12, 1885 - Jan. 14, 1953

N. Lee Samuel
Feb. 28, 1881 - Apr. 18, 1943

Ida Doggett Samuel
Sept. 22, 1886 - May 23, 1956

Baby Samuel
Jul. 9, 1930 - Jul. 11, 1930

Lucy Southworth Noel
Died May 8, 1941

Henry T. Doggett
Nov. 14, 1901 - Jan. 15, 1939

Mary Doggett Rice
Apr. 13, 1862 - Jul. 3, 1941
Son B.P. Doggett

William F. Robinson
1852-1919

Lee D. Robinson
1860-1933

Mr. John Richardson
Mr. Willkie Adams
Mrs. Willkie Adams

Sp. 1st Class S.D. Campbell
Died Oct. 2, 1951
Age 26

Two Unmarked Graves

Robert Bernard Covington
Died Jan. 8, 1961

Lloyd E. Covington
Dec. 1, 1890 - May 11, 1956

St. Paul's United Methodist Church

Earl R. Carneal
California
Pvt. Co. A, 184 Infantry
World War II
Jan. 27, 1907 - Jul. 12, 1957

John W. Carneal
Sept. 2, 1912 - Apr. 3, 1952

[Mrs. Joe Pitts]

[Mr. Joe Pitts]

[Frank Traham, mother, daughter and
niece, in walled section, unmarked]

Elizabeth J. Barlow
wife of William H. Covington
Mar. 27, 1873 - Oct. 18, 1912

Mrs. Nannie Covington
Sept. 24, 1852 - Jul. 27, 1901

William Hiter Covington
Oct. 16, 1852 - Jul. 12, 1916

Mattie J. Donahoe
Aug. 6, 1870 - Sept. 8, 1933
Star & Crescent Council No. 6
S. & D. of L.

Edna P.
wife of E.G. Donahoe
Nov. 24, 1874 - Oct. 18, 1930

Raymond Forrester Donahoe
Died Jan. 30, 1961
Age 49 yrs.

St. Peter's Episcopal Church

Located in the little town of Port Royal, Virginia, east of King Street and near the banks of the Rappahannock River. The congregation had its beginning some 20 years before the building was finished in December 1835. Bishop Richard C. Moore, of St. George's Episcopal Church of Fredericksburg, consecrated the new church on Sunday, May 15, 1836. Rev. William Friend, who lies buried in the churchyard here, became the first minister.

Born in Massachusetts in 1806, Rev. Friend attended the Virginia Theological Seminary at Alexandria before coming to Caroline County in 1833 to minister at the newly constructed Grace Episcopal Church at Corbin, Virginia. During his 38 years in the County, Rev. Friend was instrumental in founding eleven Episcopal Churches in this and the surrounding counties. His funeral was held in St. Peter's Church on May 17, 1870, and he became the first to be buried in the churchyard. Psalm 37:37 is quoted on his tombstone.

The early records of this church were destroyed by soldiers during the Civil War. The large silver chalice used by Bishop Moore in 1836 remains with the congregation today. Bishop Meade described his visit to this church in June 1837.

The brick church was severely damaged in December 1849 by fire, and had to be extensively restored. At that time, the brick was stuccoed and a second bell was placed in the steeple. This bell was later moved into the yard of the church which is now the cemetery.

This site was visited December 2, 1961.

Henrietta Pendleton
wife of George Taylor
Dec. 23, 1840 - Oct. 11, 1919

Ruth Turner
Sept. 17, 1905 - Jul. 5, 1906

Edw. Jaquelin Ware
Aug. 8, 1892 - Nov. 3, 1896

Augustine Bowen
son of George & Mary Cary Turner
Nov. 25, 1902 - June 22, 1903

Elizabeth Montgomery
wife of Rev. S.S. Ware
June 13, 1850 - Nov. 21, 1914

Rev. William Friend

Died May 16th 1870 in his 64th year

Nellie Love
only child of Dr. Charles & Louisa C.
Urquhart
Jul. 11, 1861 - Nov. 9, 1877

Charles U.
son of Rev. J.J. & Lydie W. Gravatt
Feb. 23, 1880 - Jul. 24, 1880

Mary Ambler Gravatt
Sept. 29, 1846 - May 16, 1929

Dr. John J. Gravatt
Nov. 27, 1817 - Sept. 23, 1886
and his wife
Mary E. Gravatt
Jul. 3, 1820 - Apr. 4, 1920

Lucie Jaqueline
wife of Hon. Ress T. Bowen
Oct. 14, 1847 - Sept. 30, 1906

Mary Rosina
wife of David B. Powers, and
daughter of Champ B. & Elizabeth G.
Thornton
Dec. 27, 1849 - Oct. 10, 1893

D.B. Powers
Apr. 24, 1834 - Jul. 5, 1910

David Breonard Powers
1875-1936

Elizabeth Gramer
wife of Champe B. Thornton, Sr.
Apr. 2, 1820 - Mar. 6, 1900

Matilda Grammer Thornton
daughter of Champe Brockenbrough
and Elizabeth Grammer Thornton
1856-1928

Lucy Brockenbrough
wife of Philip Wade Thornton
1797 - May 20, 1875

Lucy Anne Thornton
Dec. 14, 1833 - Mar. 1901

Charlotte Thornton
wife of Richard Ball Mitchell
Mar. 16, 1838 - Mar. 17, 1917

Loula Thornton Mitchell
Feb. 4, 1873 - March 9, 1898

Louise Disney Thornton
Feb. 3, 1877 - Jan. 27, 1933

John Tayloe Thornton
Dec. 18, 1854 - Jan. 28, 1915

John Tayloe Thornton, Jr.
Apr. 12, 1903 - June 23, 1903

Wm. T. Holloway
Died Oct. 5, 1936

Robert Green [Holloway], M.D.
1832-1919
Eliza Amiss [Holloway]
1845-1928

Patsie Julia Catlett
1845-1922
Elise Fitzhugh Catlett
1847-1933
daughters of Elizabeth Fitzhugh and
George Washington Catlett

Anna Gordon Catlett
Mar. 15, 1844 - Jul. 17, 1924

Geo. Buckner Farish
May 15, 1852 - Jan. 6, 1929

His wife
Fannie Amiss
Dec. 12, 1846 - Sept. 6, 1928

Charles Randolph
son of Charles and Randolph Powers
Jan. 25, 1920 - Jul. 21, 1941

Gilbert B. Gibbs
Nov. 4, 1861 - Mar. 5, 1916

Aubrey G. Gibbs
Feb. 23, 1885 - Sept. 14, 1915

Alice G. Gibbs
Nov. 2, 1854 - Aug. 7, 1920

John Bernard
son of Philip and Sallie S. Lightfoot
Born in Port Royal, Va., Dec. 24, 1814
Died Jul. 10, 1888

Sallie Virginia
Fourth daughter of John B. and Harriet A.
Lightfoot
Born May 25, 1856
Died in Port Royal, Va., Aug. 25, 1895

St. Peter's Episcopal Church

Harriet Ann
wife of John B. Lightfoot
Born June 28, 1822
Died in Port Royal, Va., June 11, 1871

George Patterson
Fourth son of John B. and Harriet A.
Lightfoot
Born in Port Royal, Va., May 27, 1858
Died June 4, 1887

Salem Baptist Church

Salem Baptist Church

Located on a hill in the village of Sparta, Virginia. This congregation originally met at another location further down from the present site near Alps, Virginia. In 1846, during the pastorate of Andrew Broaddus I, the church split over temperance. Part of the congregation left the original church and moved to Sparta where they built another church, naming it Mt. Calvary Church. Andrew Broaddus became pastor of the new congregation, which numbered about 200 members. At the death of his father Andrew Broaddus I, the young minister was called in 1848 to also serve as the pastor of the old church near Alps. Less than 10 years after its organization, Mt. Calvary disbanded and the members of the two churches united to form the present Salem Baptist Church at Sparta.

The cemetery is to the rear of the church. This site was visited on December 2, 1961.

William W. Butler
June 9, 1870 - Jan. 29, 1955

Fairfield W. Butler
Dec. 31, 1881 - Sept. 20, 1909

Eliza G. Butler
Feb. 16, 1843 - Mar. 20, 1920

William F. Beazley
Aug. 15, 1851 - Aug. 11, 1925

Emma J.A. Beazley
Feb. 22, 1862 - Apr. 3, 1944

SORRELL
James B. Sorrell
July 9, 1868 - Jan. 10, 1948
Ellen P. Sorrell
July 18, 1866 - Apr. 27, 1936
Viola S. Parker
Aug. 11, 1894 - Feb. 10, 1918

BROADDUS
Mordecai R. Broaddus
1807-1859
Sarah Ann Broaddus
1811-1887
John P. Broaddus
1838-1912
Susie S. Broaddus
1846-1886

William B. Kidd
1835-1875
[should be 1828-1875]

Lewis George Pitts
July 19, 1891 - May 19, 1951

Eugene Llewellyn Broaddus, M.D., C.S.A.
1839-1862
Jeanette Julia Broaddus
1842-1865
Sallie B. Snead
1844-1870

Arthur W. Loving
Oct. 31, 1877 - Sept. 6, 1950

Bertie T. Loving
June 28, 1882 -

Maxie Gregg Broaddus, Sr.
Nov. 12, 1862 - Nov. 9, 1946

Maggie L. Smoot
wife of Maxie Gregg Broaddus, Sr.
Apr. 7, 1867 - Aug. 29, 1928

Infant son of Maxie and Maggie Broaddus
Jan. 8, 1910

147

Salem Baptist Church

PULLER
James F. Puller
July 5, 1869 - Aug. 5, 1959
Glenmore Puller
July 25, 1877 - May 6, 1945

John Leland Motley
Feb. 15, 1827 - Oct. 20, 1891

Maria Broaddus Motley
Mar. 31, 1837 - Apr. 15, 1908

Laura Motley Puller
Apr. 14, 1863 - Aug. 21, 1937

Joseph Benjamin Carter
Mar. 6, 1894 - Oct. 18, 1952

Annie Ross Carter
dau. of E.P. & Ida R. Carter
Mar. 20, 1885 - July 10, 1892

Mary S. Carter
Dec. 24, 1851 - Oct. 9, 1924

Eugene P. Carter
July 3, 1849 - Mar. 15, 1928

Mattie L. Carter
Nov. 9, 1889 - May 3, 1924

Aubrey E. Carter
Dec. 14, 1891 - Jul. 13, 1935
[Mason]

Pearl C. Jones
wife of A.B. Jones
Apr. 26, 1901 - May 18, 1943

Esther Lee Carter
May 19, 1875 - Jul. 19, 1943

Eugene Carter
Jan. 29, 1862 - Nov. 7, 1952

Mother
Sallie B. Seal
Jul. 18, 1864 - Jan. 24, 1934

Elsie V. Carter
Sept. 15, 1912 - Jan. 15, 1919

Florence B. Carter
May 10, 1880 - Oct. 27, 1943

Phillip Henry Carter
Died Mar. 29, 1958
age 82 yrs. 3 mos. 4 days

Reuben A. Sorrell
1874-1944

Robert S. Chinault
1841-1906

Mary J. Chinault
1839-1919

Reuben B. Garnett
1862-1949

Laura E. Garnett
1868-1950

Henry Jasper Garnett
Apr. 24, 1892 - Oct. 21, 1928

Benjamin Franklin Broaddus
June 7, 1870 - Nov. 8, 1928

Mable Alice Broaddus
Feb. 3, 1872 - Mar. 15, 1926

Infant son of Benjamin F. & Mable
Broaddus
July 30, 1907

Infant son of Benjamin F. & Mable
Broaddus
Aug. 7, 1913

Martha J. Broaddus
1836 - June 1921

Brother James
Son of C.E. & J.H. Kay
Died Sept 2, 1904
Aged 16 yrs.

Salem Baptist Church

Challonia E. Kay
May 20, 1856 - July 24, 1913

James H. Kay
July 19, 1857 - Mar. 21, 1944

William Hamilton Kay
Sept. 28, 1882 - Mar. 7, 1960

Otho P. Beazley
Sept. 17, 1876 - Sept. 6, 1946

Maude B. Beazley
Mar. 28, 1882 - Jan. 19, 1950

Lloyd C. Beazley
June 5, 1912 - Dec. 3, 1944

Katherine B. Beazley
May 11, 1910 - May 18, 1914

Maurice F. Beazley
1868-1916
Rosa A. Beazley
1867-1927
Jessie S. Beazley
1898-1932
Raymond W. Beazley
1902-
Bernice G. Jordon
1893-

Latimer L., Jr.
son of L.L. & M.B. Beasley
Dec. 6, 1923 - Jul. 5, 1924

George Willard Kay
Aug. 3, 1886 - June 9, 1936

Mother
Sallie Gouldin (Pitts)
Aug. 12, 1885 - July 27, 1947

John H. Pitts
July 18, 1917 - Aug. 25, 1932

Lucille S. Pitts
Jan. 27, 1915 - Dec. 26, 1920

Infant son of C.M. & Sallie Pitts

Jefferson D. Pitts
1861-1931

Mollie K. Pitts
1867-1924

James Edward Moore
July 9, 1877 - Apr. 19, 1959

Mother
Susan E. Moore
Dec. 13, 1844 - Apr. 22, 1924

Father
William S. Moore
Aug. 18, 1836 - Jan. 3, 1924

Annie L. Derieux
May 8, 1894 - Sept. 29, 1905

Elizabeth K. Derieux
Aug. 23, 1869 - Jan. 18, 1945

James R. Derieux
Aug. 2, 1867 - July 18, 1951

John Cook Andrews
Mar. 21, 1897 - Oct. 24, 1953

Frederick H. Andrews
Co. D, 316 Infantry
Sept. 9, 1897 - Oct. 8, 1918

Ida B. Andrews
Nov. 27, 1869 - Oct. 3, 1952

Frederick J. Andrews
Apr. 2, 1861 - Feb. 24, 1933

George Warren Beazley
1882-1950

Wayland Lee Beazley
1885-1952

Ethel Steilen Beazley
1890-1944

149

Salem Baptist Church

Father
E. Burton Loving
Oct. 8, 1863 - June 16, 1950

Mother
Mary E. Loving
June 6, 1876 - Mar. 10, 1949

Alpheus Brooks
Mar. 5, 1868 - Sept. 14, 1948

Hauzie Haynes Brooks
Oct. 10, 1873 - May 30, 1948

Samuel Edward Ball
Nov. 26, 1893 - Feb. 25, 1950

Jetty T. Carter
Nov. 11, 1885 - Mar. 14, 1957

Samuel E. Pitts, Sr.
Sparta, Caroline County, Va.
Aug. 22, 1852 - Jan. 8, 1930

Otho C. Chenault
Nov. 18, 1878 - May 26, 1959

Hausie G. Chenault
Sept. 10, 1883 -

Lucy Tarrant Kidd
1881-1950

John Edwin Kidd
1873-1932

James Monroe Bell
Jul. 2, 1927 - July 2, 1946

Fannie Elliott Martin
Born May 22, 1872
Died Mar. 9, 1954
Age 81 yrs. 9 mos. 17 days

Infant son of Mr. & Mrs. Kyle Carter
Died Oct. 21, 1958
Age 0 yrs. 0 mos. 0 days

Alfred Chenault III
Dec. 6, 1956 - Mar. 23, 1958

William Butler Chenault
Oct. 30, 1873 - Oct. 5, 1952

Mary Garnett Chenault
Mar. 29, 1874 -

William E. Poynor
June 20, 1884 - Apr. 10, 1947

Annie G. Poynor
Apr. 5, 1887 -

Joseph A. Ball
July 26, 1883 - Sept. 17, 1947

Mother*
Mary E. Pitts
Apr. 19, 1818 - Apr. 10, 1891

Father*
Dandridge Pitts
Oct. 25, 1825 - Dec. 27, 1891

James William Taylor
Dec. 29, 1901 - Dec. 11, 1944

Helen Pickett P. Taylor
July 3, 1903 -

Maxine Taylor
May 11, 1928 - Jan. 9, 1939

Pearl Taylor
Aug. 20, 1926 - Nov. 24, 1928

William Anderson Beazley
Jan. 23, 1921 - Feb. 17, 1939

Clara M. Beazley
May 14, 1926 - May 26, 1926

---

*Graves moved twice. First buried at the Pitts homestead, later Chenault's place, moved from there in the 1890's to Samuel "Sam" Pitts place, then in the 1940's moved to Salem Church.

Salem Baptist Church

Lewis C. Beazley
Born Mar. 30, 1911
Died Dec. 23, 1939

BEAZLEY
Robert A.
Nov. 11, 1876 - Feb. 9, 1958
Florence A.
Aug. 2, 1883 - June 15, 1955

William Algernon Fraughnaugh
1906-1919

Algernon Fraughnaugh
1871-1926*
Hattie Wane, His Wife
1878-19

James Beazley
Sept. 20, 1838 - July 25, 1915

Mother
Mary Louise
wife of James Beazley
June 11, 1842 - July 9, 1927

John Robert Moore
Mar. 3, 1876 - June 30, 1953

Ellie R. Southworth**
March 9, 1872 - July 24, 1920

J.G. Broaddus
1863-1938

J. Waller Gouldin
Mar. 10, 1868 -

Lucy Emily Gouldin
May 28, 1876 - May 1, 1947

J. Edgar Gouldin
1853-1937

Roderick B. Gouldin***
1863-1935

Ruby Loving Bullock
Oct. 28, 1918 - Feb. 17, 1958

Alice Loving
wife of W. David Garrett
June 11, 1921 - Nov. 4, 1960

William David, Jr.
son of W. David & Alice W. Garrett
Nov. 7, 1947 - Feb. 6, 1956

Herbert Loving
1861-1943

Son
Joseph Payne Beazley
May 1, 1903 - Dec. 15, 1964

Eustice Farmer
Oct. 27, 1898 - May 26, 1953

Richard Lee Turberville Beale
Nov. 27, 1891 - Jan. 14, 1959

Stuart Rolph
Oct. 7, 1898 - Jan. 31, 1939

Phillips Rolph
Apr. 1, 1865 - Nov. 19, 1910

Maude J. Rolph
Jan. 2, 1864 - Mar. 15, 1945

Baby
[Marked by Stone Without Inscription]

Harriet W. Rolph
Oct. 15, 1863 - May 12, 1930

Elizabeth W. Rolph
Apr. 14, 1862 - Jul. 30, 1942

Moses Rolph
July 25, 1835 - Feb. 5, 1915
Heylie Rolph
Reuben Rolph
Harry Rolph

*Obituary in The Caroline Progress gives
December 1928 as death date.
**Grave moved from Stanhope at Kidd's
Fork.
***Obituary in The Caroline Progress
gives 1934 as death year.

Salem Baptist Church

Otho P. Campbell, M.D.
Jan. 21, 1913 - June 2, 1941

E.G. Pitts
Jan. 19, 1857 - Jan. 20, 1924

M. Victoria Pitts
Mar. 22, 1865 - Aug. 1, 1938

Chester N. Pitts
Jan. 3, 1851 - Dec. 8, 1929

John E. Pitts
Sept. 28, 1877 - Jul. 14, 1935

Robert Lee Upshaw
Mar. 20, 1863 - Mar. 26, 1944

Emma Kidd Upshaw
Dec. 20, 1875 - Dec. 29, 1951

Burnie U. Ancarrow
Apr. 23, 1859 - Mar. 2, 1936

Andrew S. Motley
1875-1943

Here Repose the Mortal Remains of the
Rev. Andrew Broaddus*
Born Nov. 4th, 1770
Died Dec. 1st, 1848

Caroline Broaddus*
wife of the late Rev. A. Broaddus
Jan. 7, 1813 - Aug. 22, 1853

Gay Broaddus
1880-1959

Lois Broaddus
1885-1958

Andrew Broaddus
1853-1926

Carrie P. Broaddus
1856-1891

Carrie Broaddus
1882-1923

Florence
wife of Richard L. Williams and daughter
of A. and M.J. Broaddus
Apr. 23, 1842 - Jul. 29, 1897

Richard Latane Williams
Oct. 11, 1837 - Mar. 7, 1907

Minnie Broaddus
1862-1943

Andrew Broaddus
May 17, 1818 - Apr. 19, 1900

Martha Jane Broaddus
Nov. 9, 1821 - Mar. 17, 1894

John Dabney Butler
May 14, 1819 - Feb. 9, 1905

Lucy E. Butler
Mar. 6, 1829 - Mar. 20, 1907

Jas. R. Richerson
1839-1898

Kate B. Richerson
1853-1917

Frank Buckner Richerson
May 17, 1878 - Oct. 6, 1947

Mattie Sutton Richerson**
Nov. 29, 1886 -

William H. Butler
March 1846 - Sept. 1896

Catherine E.
wife of James Wright
Feb. 12, 1818 - Aug. 17, 1852

---

*Grave moved in the 1920's from site of
Old Salem Church near Alps, Virginia.
**Still living. Perhaps the oldest living
person ever in Caroline.

Salem Baptist Church

Rev. J.W. Atkinson, Pastor of Mr. Calvary
Baptist Church
Died June 13, 1851, in the 28th year of
his age, a son of Temperance
Member of Leonidas Division No. 108

Robinette [Murray]
wife of
Christopher Columbus Broaddus
Born July 2, 1841
Died Mar. 13, 18__

John Henry Sylvia
July 1, 1881
Oct. 9, 1950

Wesley Lewis Loving
Aug. 10, 1944 - Feb. 19, 1950

PITTS
Willie Lee, Sr.
Aug. 27, 1889 - July 11, 1950
Myrtie Green
Nov. 3, 1893 -

GOULDIN
John William, Sr.
May 15, 1851 - June 22, 1942
Sallie Motley
Feb. 24, 1859 - Feb. 7, 1950

John William Gouldin, Jr.
November 22, 1888 - May 14, 1941

In Memory of
David Terrell Lewis
April 26, 1946

Jacob Astor Catlett
Oct. 26, 1925 - Dec. 3, 1931

John Rufus Puller
March 3, 1881 - April 4, 1931

Jennie V. Puller
March 1, 1884 - Jan. 13, 1931

Rhonda Gay
Daughter of
Eugenia P. & James R. Cecil
Mar. 9, 1858 - May 10, 1959

Emma A. Anderson
Feb. 14, 1846
Dec. 8, 1919

Maurice Allen, Jr.
May 25, 1927 - May 28, 1928

J.G. Broaddus
1863-1938

PULLER
Reuben T.
1873-1955
Gertrude F.
1879-1916

Olive Samuel
1887-1915

Gertrude Gresham Samuel
1851-1913

Ashby Gresham Samuel
1892-1913

THOMAS
Joseph Irving
Dec. 4, 1892 - Nov. 2, 1942
Sale Gouldin
Aug. 15, 1906 -

Joseph I. Thomas
Virginia
Sgt. Hq. Det. 80 Division
World War I
Dec. 4, 1892 - Nov. 2, 1942
[duplicate]

BILLUPS
Harvey B.
Feb. 21, 1867 - June 25, 1958
Clara S.
Sept. 26, 1874 -

153

Salem Baptist Church

FULLER
Arthur Lafayette
1875-
Alice Samuel
1885-1924

Harriet Gouldin Fuller*
1876-1902

Anne Green Fuller*
1845-1914

George Washington Fuller*
1849-1930

Anna Gouldin Fuller
1900-1984

Rhoda P. Friedrich
1908-1989

PULLER
James F.
July 5, 1869 - Aug. 5, 1959
Flenmore
July 25, 1877 - May 6, 1945

Sam Gresham Jones
1886-1958

Smith J.R. Bell
Born June 19, 1884
Died Sept. 19, 1923

Dora McDonald
Apr. 20, 1882 - Feb. 2, 1920

John Wesley Bell
Born Jan. 17, 1851
Died May 2, 1913

Jannette A. Bell
wife of
John Wesley Bell
Born Mar. 30, 1851
Died July 18, 1924

Alma Puller Cole
Daughter of
Lee Puller & Lillian Kidd
Oct. 12, 1891 - Oct. 8, 1931

Charles D. Loving
April 5, 1937 - Sept. 5, 1954

Arthur Geyde Loving
Sept. 30, 1915 - Feb. 1, 1938

Four graves: John W. Tucker, Fannie
Tucker, Pauline Loving, and Randolph
Tucker, were moved from Camp A.P. Hill
area to the Tucker section at Salem
Baptist Church in 1942.

---

*Graves moved from the cemetery on the
old Green family property near the home
of Arthur Fuller, and up the road several
miles from the church.

154

Site of Old Salem Baptist Church

Located 1.9 miles southwest of Alps, Virginia, on the west side of Route 618.

Salem Baptist Church was formally organized in 1802, but its actual history dates back to the "Great Revival" which spread across Virginia in 1788. This congregation first met under a brush arbor 6 miles from Sparta, Virginia, until a crude wooden structure was built in 1802 on the site of that arbor. Without a stove or a ceiling to this building, it served until it was replaced by another frame structure. In 1852, a handsome and commodious brick edifice was erected on the site, and served the congregation until it moved to its present site at Sparta.

After the site ceased to be used as a church, some of the graves, including that of Rev. Andrew Broaddus I, were moved to the new site at Sparta. The foundations of the old church still exist, and a few tombstones surround it to mark the hallowed spot. Some family lots were enclosed with iron fences. Sometime in the 1950's, two flat tombstones were stolen from the Motley family lot.

The present building site and cemetery is overgrown in running ivy and underbrush. Although there are only a few tombstones remaining, and many graves which are now barely discernable, it is quite evident that there were once many buried here. There is evidence that many of the tombstones have fallen and have been covered by growth. The last person known to have been buried here was Mrs. Richard F. Broaddus, shortly after 1903. Also buried here was the Rev. Andrew Broaddus, born November 4, 1770, died December 1, 1848, and his wife Caroline Broaddus, born January 7, 1813, died August 22, 1853. They were moved to the new Salem Church cemetery in the 1920's. Also, according to local historian Mary Elizabeth Pitts, Reverend Robert Walker Cole (Sept. 1812 - Sept. 16, 1868), who was a minister at Salem, and his fourth wife were buried at Salem in the lot with Andrew Broaddus I. The records of Miss Pitts also show two other graves in this cemetery, with dates but no names as follows: October 25, 1825 - December 27, 1891, and April 19, 1818 - April 10, 1891.

From this site in 1854, about 200 persons set out in a wagon train, stretching one mile in length, for Texas as homesteaders. They settled in the vicinity of Caldwell, Texas where they built a church named Salem. A marker was dedicated there in 1971 to commemorate Judge Andrew S. Broaddus who led the group to Texas.

Also buried here are: Mordecai Redd Broaddus, born 1807, died May 29, 1859; his wife Sarah Ann Miller Broaddus, born 1811, died September 24, 1877; their daughter Miss Sussie S. Broaddus, born February 17, 1846, died August 24, 1886; William Boutwell Kidd, son of Captain William Kidd and Harriet M. Wright of Kidds Fork, born December 22, 1828, died December 27, 1875 (he was the husband of Attaway "Attie" Broaddus, another daughter of Mordecai Redd Broaddus and wife Sarah Ann Miller); Attaway Broaddus, born February 29, 1836, died August 6, 1916 in Richmond where she was buried in Riverview cemetery. A stone has been placed in the cemetery of Salem Church at Sparta, in memory of the four sited above; however, the date of birth for William B. Kidd is in error.

155

Site of Old Salem Baptist Church

This site was visited in 1953, and again in 1962.

Thomas Motley
February 24, 1810 - April 6, 1868

Catherine Ann
wife of Thomas Motley
September 15, 1811 - June 3, 1846

Sally Ann
daughter of Nathaniel and Lucy Motley
Born August 10, 1828
Married R. Green, February 3, 1857
Died September 26, 1873

Richard F. Broaddus
2nd Lt. Co. H, 30 Va. Inf., C.S.A.

Virginia M. Henshaw
wife of Richard F. Broaddus

Alice B.
wife of W.J. Collins
Born August 15, 1846
Died June 14, 1876

Jos. W.
son of W.J. and Alice B. Collins
Died October 20, 1872
Age 7 mos.

In Memory of Columbia
Born May 7, 1849
Died December 4, 1860
Mabel
Born February 3, 1857
Died November 26, 1857
Everett
Born June 23, 1860
Died February 12, 1861
Children of
A. & M.J. Broaddus

Shiloh Methodist Church

Located at Bagby, Virginia, on Route 627, now Mattaponi Trail. Organized in 1832, the original meeting house was built on an acre of land donated by Silas J. Broaddus. In 1885, a new church building was erected which still serves the congregation. The old building was given to Woodford S. Broaddus who used it as a barn until it was destroyed by high winds a few years ago. The work on the new church was done mostly by members, and the timbers were cut by hand. Services were held in the new church even before its completion. The appearance of the church is simple and in good taste, and has not been altered since its construction.

This site was visited on July 8, 1961.

Mattie Shepherd
wife of M.W. Gayle of Richmond, Va.
Born Sept. 24, 1854
Died Jul. 9, 1884

J.T. Upshaw
Died Nov. 13, 1928

Virginia Upshaw
Born 1857
Died Mar. 3, 1942

L.A.C.
[Mrs. L.A. Chenault]

Lawrence B. Seal
May 19, 1847
Mar. 7, 1917
Gabriella H. Pruett
Dec. 8, 1843
May 13, 1917

SEAL
Charles R.
Feb. 20, 1876
May 17, 1944
Alice E.
Sept. 11, 1872
Dec. 28, 1954

Eugene Earl Beasley
May 25, 1913
Sept. 2, 1916

William Gravatt
1860-1921

Myrtle Gravatt
1871-1930

William W. Kidd
Sept. 30, 1879
Jul. 3, 1953

Daisy B. Kidd
Nov. 8, 1880
Jul. 13, 1937

Ethel Mead Broaddus
Jan. 27, 1879
Dec. 1, 1921

James Irvin Broaddus
Nov. 30, 1839
Nov. 8, 1918

Annie Broaddus Upshaw
Jan. 28, 1866
May 19, 1945

William Gwathmey
only son of Joseph Thomas and Mozelle
Broaddus Kidd
Nov. 27, 1907
June 19, 1918

Shiloh Methodist Church

Mozelle B. Kidd
July 16, 1881
May 6, 1923

Joseph T. Kidd
Sept. 12, 1870
Jan. 14, 1950

Ida C. Broaddus*
Born May 7, 1855
Died July 23, 1924

William Gravatt
1860-1921

Myrtle Gravatt
1871-1930

Pattye B. Gouldin
May 20, 1881
Apr. 9, 1945

Alfred B.
son of R.B. & P.B. Gouldin
Jul. 13, 1904
Feb. 20, 1908

Stuart Broaddus Richardson
Jan. 31, 1925
May 19, 1925

Woodford Broaddus
1844-1920

Mollie Wright Broaddus
1852-1926

Mattie S. Dyson
Dec. 4, 1867
Jul. 10, 1947

John W[illiam]. Dyson
Oct. 2, 1858
Aug. 15, 1920

Emma Jane Mundie
Jul. 18, 1883
Dec. 29, 1949

Unmarked Grave
[sister of Emma Jane and 2nd wife of Jeff
Mundie]

In a fenced section in back of the church:

Willie [Dunn]
Born Aug. 20, 1871
Died March 11, 1907
Mama [Dunn]
Born June 6, 1937
Died March 1, 1906

Andrew J. Dunn
Co. K
30 Regt.
Va. Inf
C.S.A.
1833-1909

In a fenced area to the left front of the church:

Brother
Thomas L. Pitts
1889-1927

Mother
Columbia F. Pitts
1854-1928

In the field near the main road:

Richard Brooks
Sgt. 47 Va. Inf., C.S.A.
July 19, 1930

---

*Obituary in The Caroline Progress gives
June 1934 as death date.

159

Wright's Chapel Methodist Church

Located on Route 639 (Ladysmith Road), about 3.2 miles east of U.S. Route 1, or about midway between U.S. Route 1 and Route 207 (Rogers Clark Boulevard).

In 1835, after meeting for a number of years at his home, William Wright gave one acre of land and had built at his own expense a small meeting house called "Wright's Chapel." Although an Episcopalian all his life, Wright united with the Methodist Church on his deathbed.

A second building which replaced the 1835 structure stood on this site until 1961 when it was demolished. At that time the congregation moved to modern brick building on a new site, located .3 mile east of U.S. Route 1 on Ladysmith Road, and 3.1 miles west of the second church site. The cemetery now marks the site of the second church. There is no cemetery at the present church site.

This site was visited July 8, 1961.

Rhoda E. Carter
wife of L.H. Carter
Born Dec. 29, 1849
Died Aug. 1, 1904

Julia A. Sonneman
wife of Geo. A. Sonneman, daughter of
L.H. and R.E. Carter
Died Dec. 26, 1902

Ernest H. Carneal
Pvt. 7 Inf. 3 Div., World War II
Born Nov. 1, 1921
Died Oct. 19, 1943

Ollie Carneal
wife of Herbert Carneal
1888-1932

Judith Raye Morris
Jul. 24, 1943
Dec. 27, 1943

Archie R. Carter
son of L.H. & R.E. Carter, husband of Ada
C. Carter
Born Oct. 16, 1874
Died May 11, 1904

Mary E. Durrett
Born Feb. 19, 1895
Died Sept. 11, 1956

James H. Durrett
Born Jul. 18, 1888
Died Feb. 13, 1955

Bettie S. Campbell
1866-1936

W. Floyd Campbell
1876-1941

Oscar H. Carneal
1880-1938

John Wallace Swisher
1884-1943

E.B. Carter
Died Dec. 15, 1945

Robertie Ann Carter
Born Sept. 15, 1864
Died Jan. 12, 1954

Joyce Ann Carneal
Born Mar. 20, 1946

Wright's Chapel Methodist Church, Original Site

Located at Balty, Virginia, this site is situated on a parcel of land which adjoins the farm of Mildred Parr, and across the road from the site of the second Wright's Chapel Methodist Church.

Near the site of this cemetery stood the home of William Wright. Methodism in Caroline County had its beginning at this house. William Wright, having been inspired by attending a service in nearby Hanover County, offered his house as a place to hold meetings. The place became known as the Methodist Chapel, or Meeting House. The first sermon was preached here in 1774.

The nearby private Wright burying ground became the Wright's Chapel cemetery. Here three of the ministers who served this church lie buried, including Luther Wright, Durrett Wright, and James Wright.

Timothy B. Seal
1849-1925

Martha T. Seal
1863-1924

Milton H. Seal
1916-1918

Douglas Dandridge Durrett
Oct. 30, 1911
Oct. 14, 1915

Eddie M. Durrett
1909-1939

Nannie B. Durrett
1887-1950

John S. Durrett
1883-1953

Mary T.
wife of W.S. Durrett
Aug. 31, 1856
Mar. 28, 1937

W.S. Durrett
husband of Mary T. Durrett
Mar. 4, 1853
June 5, 1942

John A. Durrette
1906-1960
[died of severe burns]

Everett A. Smith
1873-1934

L. Berry Wright
Mar. 11, 1858
Nov. 14, 1936

Sadie Smith Wright
Oct. 8, 1878
Feb. 19, 1951

Cicero Burruss
1865-1944

Elizabeth Spencer Burruss
Sept. 28, 1872
Jan. 3, 1929

Lucye Pleasant Burruss Osborne
Died Dec. 28, 1944

Mack Cabbell Osborne
June 14, 1881
Mar. 9, 1955

Adelaide (Addie) O. Burruss
Died June 23, 1951

162

Wright's Chapel Methodist Church, Original Site

George T. Carneal
Sept. 1879
Nov. 28, 1947

Mrs. Ann Carneal Acors
Died Feb. 23, 1961
age 69 yrs.

Johnnie W. Cannon
Jul. 10, 1906
Feb. 8, 1950

Clarence W. Cannon
Dec. 1, 1944
Jan. 15, 1950

Alvin W. Cannon
Feb. 2, 1941
Jan. 15, 1950

Welford E. Cannon
Dec. 9, 1937
Jan. 15, 1950

[3 previous killed by train at Penola
crossing]

James Jackson Reynolds
1865-1945

Lennie Satterwhite Reynolds
1870-1940

F. Daniel Satterwhite
1872-1912

Susan Carneal Satterwhite
1850-1910

John W. Satterwhite
1845-1906

James D. Wright, Jr.
Nov. 12, 1854
Aug. 23, 1889

James Durrett Wright
Mar. 1826
Apr. 18, 1898

Mrs. Maggie Coghill
Died May 3, 1959
aged 83 yrs. 10 mos. 8 days

William H. Seal
1881-1949

Elinor
daughter of J. and S. Durrett
Died Aug. 23, 1915
age 10 mos.

Sadie Acors
wife of Japheth Durrett
Died Jan. 1, 1918
age 31 yrs.

John F. Durrett
Oct. 13, 1858
Feb. 5, 1929

Bettie O. Durrett
1856-1915

William W. Carneal, Sr.
July 3, 1895
Nov. 12, 1943

Minnie J. Evans
1891-1950

Manly Broaddus Seal
Sept. 19, 1883
Nov. 6, 1957
Husband of
Lula Garvin
Born Mar. 7, 1898

John B. Seal
Aug. 25, 1852
Mar. 4, 1927

Frances E. Seale
Aug. 26, 1823
May 15, 1890

Cornelius T. Durrett
Dec. 15, 1889
Oct. 20, 1904

163

Wright's Chapel Methodist Church, Original Site

James E. Carneal
1885-1949

Bettie E. Carneal
Dec. 26, 1909
July 22, 1912

J. Henry Durrett
June 30, 1821
Aug. 26, 1859

Catharine E. Durrett
Aug. 24, 1825
Apr. 28, 1881

Bettie E. Durrett
Dec. 18, 1850
May 18, 1885

Lola S. Donahoe
June 20, 1876
Jul. 27, 1939

John G. Donahoe
Dec. 10, 1874
June 26, 1934

William B. Wright
May 11, 1846
Dec. 16, 1928

Alfred Wright
Aug. 17, 1853
Dec. 7, 1928

Ann Jane Swann
wife of Dr. Wesley Wright
Mar. 9, 1823
Nov. 19, 1909

Dr. Wesley Wright
Apr. 8, 1799
Sept. 13, 1879

Mary Ann Green
wife of Dr. Wesley Wright and daughter
of James White and Elizabeth, his wife
Aug. 29, 1816
July 9, 1855

Wesley Wright
Apr. 21, 1844
Aug. 26, 1911

Lizzie Butler
wife of Wesley Wright
May 14, 1856
Oct. 28, 1916

J. Raymond Wright
Dec. 14, 1895
Aug. 16, 1916

Jesse O. Barker
1894-1955

Maude V. Barker
1901-1941

Ella Durrette Satterwhite
May 9, 1880
May 24, 1955

Richard Joseph Satterwhite
July 1, 1873
Mar. 30, 1938

Jessie T. Satterwhite
June 13, 1911
Aug. 18, 1953

Marcena W. Head
June 29, 1791
Sept. 3, 1878

Elizabeth Esther Head
Apr. 6, 1839
Dec. 7, 1915

Archer O. Head
July 31, 1877
Oct. 6, 1878

Lucy Lee Head
Jul. 31, 1877
Dec. 10, 1877

Rachel F.W. Head
Nov. 12, 1869
Aug. 2, 1872

Wright's Chapel Methodist Church, Original Site

Joseph Wesley Jerrell
Aug. 13, 1852
Jul. 20, 1953

James W. Jerrell
born in Stafford Co., Va.
Aug. 14, 1831
Nov. 4, 1861

Luther W. Jerrell
born in Stafford Co., Va.
Born Jan. 1, 1844 - wounded in battle on
the Boydton Plank Road, Dinwiddie Co.,
Va., Oct. 27, 1864
Died at Sutherland Station, S.S.R.R.,
Oct. 31, 1864

Rachael Wright Jerrell
Dec. 1, 1849
Nov. 26, 1897

James S. Jerrell
Feb. 19, 1800
Dec. 19, 1879

Caroline Virginia Jerrell
June 18, 1837
Aug. 23, 1911

Deborah Ann Jerrell
born in Stafford Co., Va.
Born July 1, 1835
Died July 9, 1914

Our Darling
Baby Son of L.J. and Lucy Head
Apr. 29, 1906
May 1, 1906

Rachel Margaret Head
Dec. 22, 1908
Dec. 21, 1918

Lucy Fox Head
Sept. 17, 1877
Aug. 11, 1944

Luther Jerrell Head, M.D.
Mar. 6, 1866
Nov. 8, 1951

Susan Terrell Wright
Nee Burruss
Born 1828
Died Sept. 12, 1851

Elizabeth Burruss
consort of Pleasant Burruss, Sr.
Mar. 9, 1795
June 20, 1863
aged 68 yrs.

Pleasant Terrell Burruss
Sept. 30, 1822
May 30, 1895

Jane F. Burruss
July 20, 1840
March 4, 1906

Clarence W. Madison
Nov. 12, 1911
Jul. 2, 1913

John W. Madison
Died March 4, 1960
age 80 yrs.

Archie Dick Carneal
Jul. 4, 1861
Aug. 8, 1936

Annie C. Carneal
Nov. 9, 1866
Mar. 28, 1904

William James Cannon
May 14, 1884
May 4, 1944

Mrs. Maddie Cannon
Died 1906

John F. Acors
June 10, 1927
Sept. 23, 1940

Frank W. Acors
Oct. 21, 899
Nov. 24, 1937

Wright's Chapel Methodist Church, Original Site

C.T. Acors

Cedon L. Acors
Jan. 20, 1905
Aug. 2, 1940

Sherman Howard "Bill" Acors*
Oct. 10, 1928
May 1, 1935

George T. Acors
Jan. 10, 1879
Nov. 28, 1947
Husband of
Mary E. Acors
Born Oct. 15, 1885

---

*Killed while walking with his mother
along the road.

INDEX

BOULWARE
  Agatha S. 55
  Andrew L. 86
  Battaile 56
  Bessie E. 61
  Caroline B. 55
  Carrie F. 61
  Dorothy 55
  Elliott 55
  Eugene 55
  Eva 73
  Frances 55
  George K. 61
  George W. 61
  James 55, 56
  James L. 55
  Landon C. 65
  Lucy 72
  Lucy J. 72
  Mark 55, 72
  Milly 55
  Molly 55
  Nellie B. 55
  Richard 55
  Sallie H. 65
  Sarah P. 72
  Sherwood W. 61
  Thomas K. 61
  Turner 55
  W.T. 72
  Willard T. 73
  William T. 72
BOWEN
  Lucie J. 144
  Ress T. 144
BOWERS
  C.E. 32
  Charles C. 32
  Emily R. 31
  Harvie 31
  J.H. 30
  James R. 31
  Margaret P. 27
  Mary C. 32
  Robert H. 31
  Sherwood C. 27
  Thomas C. 30
  Wallace E. 31
  William S. 31
BOWIE
  Ada L. 62
  Charles J. 62

Eugene 63
Eugene M. 63
Fannie P. 62
Frank E. 46
H. Corbin 62
Julia I. 63
Lucy V. 62
Sophia H. 63
Walter N. 62
Willie D. 62
Willing 63
Bowling Green
    Methodist
    Church 98
BRADLEY
  James I. 59
  Martha T. 59
  Thornton H. 60
  Virginia E. 64
BRAME
  Joseph 27
BRAULT
  Alice L. 112
  Ernest E. 112
BROADDUS
  A. 152, 156
  A. Baynham 62
  Alice M. 90, 92
  Andrew 152, 155
  Andrew S. 155
  Anne W. 92
  Benjamin F. 148
  Bernice W. 53
  Blanche E. 105
  Caroline 152, 155
  Caroline G. 92
  Carrie 152
  Carrie M. 105
  Carrie P. 152
  Charles A. 105
  Chrissie R. 56
  Christine 56
  Christopher C. 153
  Columbia 156
  Cornelius C. 56
  Dora D. 67
  Elizabeth 54
  Ella N. 96
  Ellen O. 54
  Emily L. 105
  Emma D. 105
  Erasmus S. 53

Erle C. 53
Ethel M. 158
Ethel N. 105
Eugene 68, 105
Eugene L. 147
Everett 156
Florence 152
Frank D. 68
G.W. 54
Gay 152
George C. 54
George W. 53
Gouldin L. 67
Ida C. 159
Infant 62, 147, 148
J.G. 151, 153
James I. 158
James J. 54
Jeanette J. 147
John G. 92
John P. 147
John R. 70
John W. 67
Kate G. 92
Lissie R. 54
Lois 152
Lucy B. 62
Lucy L. 67
M.J. 152, 156
Mabel 156
Mabel P. 67
Mable A. 148
Madalaine T. 103
Maggie L. 147
Martha J. 68, 148,
    152
Martha T. 91
Mary M. 92
Maxie G. 147
Melville T. 96
Minnie 152
Mollie W. 159
Mordecai R. 147
Nellie G. 70
Ophie E. 54
Pauline G. 86
Richard B. 103
Richard F. 155,
    156
Robinette 153
S.W. 105
Sarah A. 147

170

174

Julia W. 87
CLAYTOR
Benjamin V. 141
Charles L. 141
Elizabeth R. 77
J. Earl 113
John W. 113
Margaret A. 141
CLENDENNEN
Clyde A. 90
CLIFT
Florence B. 71
COATES
Family 81
Oliver G. 24
COBB
A.L. 22
E.C. 22
Lannie A. 22
Lloyd 22
COFFEY
Alice H. 18
Charles L. 18
Dewey 18
Frances H. 39
John F. 39
Lloyd W. 18
Mattie M. 18
COGHILL
Annie W. 105
B.K. 91
C.S. 91
C.W. 91
E.R. 91
E.S. 91
Fannie E. 10
Florence A. 10
H.B. 105
Isla S. 24
Joseph D. 8
Lou L. 105
Maggie 163
Mary B. 8
Mary C. 105
Pleasant B. 24
Rena C. 8
Robert A. 105
Rosa 105
Sym. G. 10
Thomas D. 105
William G. 105

COLAW
Nora B. 125
Wilbur D. 125
COLE
Alma P. 154
Mor. W. 52
Robert W. 155
COLEMAN
Burnley G. 68
C.F. 104
Caddie D. 7
Douglas 21
Edna F. 6
Emmett M. 6
Florence 136
Frederick W. 6
H.F. 6
Hugh K. 6
James L. 103
Jennie M. 6
John R. 8
Lucy H. 21
M. Eulalia 69
Minnie B. 87
Minnie L. 87
Rebecca J. 99
Robin S. 6
Solon T. 6
Willie E. 2
COLLAWN
Elenora 65
Ena W. 74
Frederick E. 65
Holloway C. 64
J.W. 65
Judith S. 65
Lelia P. 64
Lottie 64
Malvonia W. 74
Maude E. 63
Mollie F. 64
R.S. 64
Robert A. 64
Thomas B. 65
Virginia E. 64
W.S. 65
Walter S. 65
William N. 64
COLLIER
Clara W. 54
COLLINS
Alice B. 156

Athol ix
Belle B. 95
Belle H. 95
Bettie L. 98
C. Ridgely 98
Charles B. 76
Charles L. 98
Chastian F. 75
E. Athol 99
E. Burke 95
Edgar B. 93
Florence B. 93
Geo. R. 99
George R. 84
George T. 94
George W. 95
Jane B. 94
Jas. R. 99
Jos. W. 156
Julia F. 36
Pearl C. 95
R.E. 95
Rebecca J. 99
Sallie 37
Susan W. 37
W. Garnett 98
W.J. 156
Collins Family Cemetery
7, 81
COLLISON
Charlie 24
Hattie J. 24
James L. 19
Joe M. 24
Willie M. 24
Concord Baptist Church
27
CONWAY
A.H. 63
Anne H. 63
Aylett H. 63
C.B. 71
Fannie H. 63
Frances K. 63
George F. 63
Laura B. 71
COOK
Alice S. 47
Davis L. 47
Elmer L. 47
F.G. 47
Frank G. 47

175

176

Benjamin W. 127
Edward J. 75
Emma 75
James B. 127
Kate 6
Mary E. 75
Mary L. 6
Minnie 6
Nannie D. 128
Pattie S. 127
Robert L. 6
Thomas J. 75
W.S. 8
William P. 127
FONDREN
Ruth B. 63
FOSTER
Carrie B. 93
FOUNTAINE
James R. 131
FOX
James P. 34
Lucy T. 118
FRANK
John S. 91
Lucy E. 91
FRAUGHNAUGH
Algernon 151
Hattie W. 151
William A. 151
FRAZIER
William E. 103
FREEMAN
Augustus M. 31
Emma D. 31
James W. 31
Mary E. 31
Robert D. 31
V.I. 31
FRENCH
Algernon S. 101
FRIEDRICH
Rhoda P. 154
FRIEND
William 143
FRITTS
Mary E. 124
FULLER
Alice S. 154
Anna G. 154
Anne G. 154
Arthur L. 154

George W. 154
Harriet G. 154
FUQUA
Virginia H. 49
FURCRON
Albert A. 33
FURR
Elizabeth J. vi

G

GABY
Albina M. 134
John 134
GACEK
John 108
GALLINGER
Annamelia S. 9
Cyrenus 9
GALYEN
C.W. 34
Infants 34
J.A. 34
Mollie Y. 34
Yancy C. 34
GAMBLE
Charles F. 74
GARLAND
Annie R. 124
Dana H. 7
Edward J. 124
Jeffrey L. 7
Ruby 7
GARNER
J. Leonard 58
GARNETT
Aubrey P. 111
Birtie B. 119
Emma A. 119
Emma S. 52
Family 83
Henry J. 148
Isabell S. 111
Jane S. 52
John W. 119
Laura E. 148
Mattie W. 80
Myrtle M. 111
Reuben B. 148
Robert L. 111
Robert S. 52

Sallie 73
Smedley 111
Walker 73
Walker J. 73
William G. 52
GARRETT
Alice L. 151
Alice W. 151
Arthur L. 67
Aubrey 93
Charles C. 80
Clarence W. 92
Ellen G. 68
Family 78
Fannie B. 73
Fleetwood 50
George E. 70
Ida A. 89
James E. 69
Jennis E. 78
John J. 69
John M. 46
Julia F. 73
Julian W. 68
Louis C. 92
Margaret J. 92
Mary 101
Mary B. 93
Mary L. 101
Montgomery G.
101
R.L. 73
Robert L. 70
Susie L. 70
W. David 151
William D. 151
William R. 69
William T. 89
Willie 50
Winston 93
GARTH
Eloise E. 62
GATEWOOD
Annah 39
Bernice L. 85
Charles J. 39
Clarence H. 3
Clifton L. 2
Emma C. 85
Estelle L. 3
General W. 85
Infant 85

179

180

181

Hopewell Methodist
   Church 83
HOUCK
   Bobby H. 3
   John P. 3
   Lila J. 3
   William A. 3
HOUSTON
   Addison L. 115
   Archie 111
   Bettie L. 80
   C.B. 47
   Calvin N. 47
   Coleman 122
   Della P. 49
   Diliah C. 47
   F.M. 47
   G.L. 49
   Grover C. 47
   Infant 20
   Joseph R. 20
   Kate L. 47
   Martha 49
   Martha E. 115
   Molly 122
   R.B. 20
   William H. 49
HOWARD
   Bettie 58
   Bly 57
   Dorothy 57
   Jim 58
   Judson 58
   Lannie 130
   Louise 57
   Maria 58
   Reubin 58
   S. Alice 57
HOY
   Mr. ix
HUDGENS
   Clifton 24
HUDGIN
   Ellen H. 101
   Jack 101
   Robert 101
   Sally G. 101
   Wescom 101
HUDSON
   John D. 104
HUFFINES
   Alice B. 56

Claude G. 56
Harold 57
HUGHES
   Deliah S. 15
   Eva T. 14
   Henry E. 15
   Henry P. 15
   Infant 14
   Robert S. 14, 15
HUMPHRIES
   C.T. 38
   Hattie W. 38
   Hawsie D. 38
   Samuel J. 38
   W.L. 38
HUNTER
   Florence C. 136
   Jas. 136
   Richard 51
HUTCHERSON
   J. Franklin 18
HUTCHESON
   Emmett H. 29
   Mollie B. 29
HUTT
   Lucelle V. 59
   Lucille V. 59
   William O. 59
HYATT
   Sadie C. 95
   Thomas O. 95

I

Infant 13, 21, 87, 151

J
J.
   J.H. 78
JACKSON
   Elizabeth W. 87
   John R. 87
   Julia W. 87
   Thomas P. 13
JAMES
   Reginald W. 128
JAMESON
   Margaret C. 99

JENKINS
   Thos. L. 132
JERRELL
   Caroline V. 165
   Deborah A. 165
   James S. 165
   James W. 165
   Joseph W. 165
   Luther W. 165
   Rachael W. 165
   Sallie D. 86
   William D. 86
Jerusalem 22
JESSE
   C. Ridgely 93
   Charles T. 93
   Joseph E. 93
   Peter T. 93
   Sarah A. 93
JESSIE
   Nannie 63
JETER
   Bessie W. 63
   Blanche B. 42
   Catherine 59
   Emma B. 27
   Eugene B. vii, 42
   Henry A. 31
   Jeremiah G. 63
   Louise A. 63
   Samuel B. 61
   Thomas B. 42
   Willie T. 61
JOHNSON
   Audrey L. 15
   Burnley 15
   Eulalia H. 42
   George B. 6
   Infant 28
   Julia I. 6
   Lucy 15
   Mary C. 15
   Thomas E. 54
   W. Earl 15
   William T. 15
JONES
   A. 79
   A.B. 148
   A.L. 98
   A.M. 79
   Alvin W. 130
   Annie H. 131

183

184

185

Richard 24
Thomas J. 74
William B. 91
MAHOLICK
Ella 138
John M. 138
MAHON
Bernard W. 90
Charles B. 90
Cora C. 90
Peggy 90
MAJERAK
Joseph 134
MAKELEY
Valentine F. 84
MANNS
Paul W. viii
MARMADUKE
Ann 82
George 82
Mary 82
MARSHALL
Andrew B. 88
Betty C. 88
Clarence W. 68
Florence G. 129
George W. 46
Glassell H. 72
Gracie C. 2
Ila M. 2
J.H. 47
John G. 47
John W. 46
Polly 46
R. Mason 2
Robert A. 2
Sallie T. 68
Sarah E. 46
Unmarked graves
47
Walter W. 2
MARTENS
Sadie B. 93
MARTIN
Aubrey L. 74
Calvin 130
David L. 75
Elizabeth 59
Ernest B. 89
Family 83
Fannie E. 150
Garnett L. 93

George 66
Gouldie L. 73
Gracie B. 96
Harry 56
Infant 56
Jesse 122
John 66
John R. 75
Joseph B. 73
Kate L. 56
Lawrence E. 85
Leroy 84
Luther H. 89
Maggie L. 73
Margaret 56
Mary Y. 74
Raymond 122
Rosa B. 113
Will I. 96
MARTOLA
Bernice G. 118
MASLANKO
John 138
Mary E. 138
MAURY
Anne F. 94
Charles W. 94
Emily L. 94
Harriet W. 94
Henry T. 94
Leonard T. 94
Rutson 94
William L. 94
MAYO
Frances K. 63
J.E. 63
Jacob E. 63
McALLISTER
Bettie L. 40
Bettie P. 40
C.A. 3
Chas. W. 108
Frank 19
Henry L. 4
Infant 40
J.R. 40
John 40
Julia 3
Nellie 19
Ryland A. 40
Virginia M. 3
Walter L. 40

McCARTHY
Hannah B. 47
Robert L. 47
McCURDY
Catherine W. 93
McDONALD
Dora 154
William W. 77
McKAY
Alma 49
William S. 49
McKENNEY
Clarence 72
Edgar 83
Eva M. 6
Everett E. 103
Fanny G. 72
Lester C. 6
Louis B. 6
Mary J. 72
Willie 72
McWHIRT
David D. 131
Eleanor S. 7
Mary P. 131
Raymond R. 7
MERCHANT
Grace E. 22
METCALF
Esther D. 98
MEYER
Clara B. 103
John H. 103
MICHALIGA
John J. 134
Theresa 134
MICOU
Georgie 71
James R. 71
Marion 71
Mary 71
MIDDLEBROOK
A. Vernon 18
Catherine D. 19
Clarence L. 19
Cornelius T. 18
Doris L. 18
J.K. 25
Leanious C. 19
Lewis W. 19
Mary C. 18
Mrs. 25

Rosa Y. 18
Sicilian W. 18
Willie C. 19
MIDDLEBROOKS
Annie 24
MILLER
Annette D. 91
William P. 91
MILLS
Andrew L. 54
B.F. 83
Benjamin F. 12
Bennie H. 128
Charlie 12
Columbia G. 12
Dorothy G. 11
E.V. 100
Edgar W. 64
Edward L. 11
Edward W. 64
Emma 83
Geneva 11
Genevieve 11
Harold 128
Infant 100
Leslie L. 11
Littleberry A. 130
Lottie C. 64
Mary G. 128
Ollie C. 128
Oscar V. 128
P.M. 100
Pallison B. 54
Taft B. 130
Tomasia J. 54
William W. 130
MINOR
John C. 58
MINTON
Ida M. 40
MITCHELL
Arlene 15
C.L. 15
C.R. 32
Charlotte T. 144
Chas. R. 32
Elijah A. 15
Everett W. 14
Infant 15
J.L. 15
John E. 28
Joseph L. 14

L.B. 15
Loula T. 144
Molly E. 32
P.B. 15
Phoebe S. 32
Richard B. 144
Rosie E. 32
Ruby S. 47
S. Dudley 14
Sarah S. 15
Victoria S. 14
William F. 32
MOLNAR
Helen 134
MONCURE
Annie E. 99
Eustace C. 99
Fanny I. 99
Richard G. 99
MOODY
Cather 33
Lillie L. 34
Wade W. 34
MOORE
Annie J. 96
Carl B. 114
George W. 57
Harry G. 96
Hauzie W. 57
James E. 149
John R. 151
Maria M. 99
Reuben B. 113
Richard C. 143
Susan E. 149
William S. 149
Willie I. 113
MOREFIELD
Clyde 124
Hattie 124
Infant 124
John H. 124
Mary E. 124
MOREN
A.L. 15
Alma T. 14
Infant 15
J. Arthur 14
M.M. 15
MORGAN
Linda A. 57

MORRIS
Esther E. 5
Irene C. 97
Joseph S. 33
Judith R. 161
Lila T. 34
Lucy C. 5
Mary E. 5
Moses H. 58
Pearl 58
Ruby M. 5
Woodrow W. 5
MORRISON
Alfred H. 27
Annie H. 27
George S. 27
MOSS
Alice H. 125
Infant 125
John 125
Moss Side 22
MOTLEY
Andrew S. 152
Catherine A. 156
Charles H. 52
Clara B. 48
Essie G. 50
Family 155
Fannie B. 52
Helen W. 48
Henry J. 47
Infant 48
John L. 148
John N. 50
Laura 67
Lizzie L. 67
Lucy 156
Maria B. 148
Martha E. 67
Nathaniel 156
Ora 67
Robert L. 71
Sally A. 156
T.H. 67
Thomas 156
Thomas H. 67
Tommie 67
Willie B. 50
MOULD
Mary E. 78
Mt. Calvary Church
147

187

189

190

191

SCRIPTURE
Margaret G. 100
Mason G. 100
Norman C. 100
Violet S. 100
SEAL
Alice E. 158
Charles R. 158
Chas. W. 74
Elizabeth L. 111
Georgianna W. 38
Irene M. 74
John B. 163
L.F. 14
Lawrence B. 158
Lula G. 163
Manly B. 163
Martha T. 162
Milton H. 162
Sallie B. 148
Timothy B. 162
V. Katherine 14
V.L. 14
Walter F. 111
William H. 163
SEALE
Frances E. 163
SEAMAN
Anna E. 7
Charles H. 7
Hervey J. 7
John P. 7
SEAY
Angelina 41
Blanche 40
Carl W. 41
Doris R. 37
Emmett 41
George G. 41
George T. 40
Ida L. 40
Infant 37
John L. 40
Marshie P. 37
Mary T. 40
Roy B. 37
Sarah S. 40
W. Russell 41
SELF
Addie V. 130
Walter F. 130
William J. 130

SELPH
Fannie 77
Frank T. 76
Jarrin 58
John 58
Joseph L. 102
Juin 58
Margaret 58
Phebe 58
Sallie 58
Stuart K. 76
Weyman R. 76
SEMPLE
R.B. 65
Virginia 65
SEYMOUR
Charlie W. 118
Jennie C. 53
Leona F. 74
SHACKELFORD
B.C. 60
Nannie W. 30
SHADDOCK
Allie 56
Annie D. 55
Betsey 55
Dora 56
Eugene 55
Fred M. 56
Frederick C. 55
Ida M. 55
James 55
Jessie A. 56
SHEHERDSON
Emma C. 117
SHELTON
Eugene 11
Fannie E. 131
James 131
Jane 11
Lillie W. 11
Richard M. 11
SHEPHERDSON
J.P. 117
Shiloh Methodist
   Church 158
SHORT
James W. 10
SHOUPE
Bessie 124
SHUMAN
Callie 114

Caroline O. 114
Charles A. 110,
   114
Ernest 114
Frank E. 116
Joseph A. 114
Nannie W. 116
Oteria E. 114
Stella M. 90
SHUPE
Stephen B. 124
SIMMONS
Emma V. 34
SIMMS
Dewey 28
Infant 28
Mildred 28
SIMPKINS
Catherine E. 84
John W. 84
Robert F. 28
SIMULCIK
Hermina 134
Jan 134
John 134
Viktor 134
SIRLES
Freddie G. 111
Lelia P. 114
Lewis L. 110, 111
Lucy A. 111
Roberta E. 114
Woodford P. 114
SITARIK
Ozef 134
SIZER
Mordica T. 37
Rosa S. 37
SKINKER
Ben M. 99
Laura J. 99
Mary B. 66
Mary G. 68
William E. 68
SKINNER
Alice G. 68
Alice J. 61
Charlie 77
Georgie E. 128
Gladys W. 128
Infant 77
James M. 132

194

196

Made in the USA
Charleston, SC
05 December 2013